kid chef junior

kid chef junior

MY *First* KIDS' COOKBOOK

Anjali Shah

PHOTOGRAPHY BY MARIJA VIDAL

R

ROCKRIDGE
PRESS

Designer: Liz Cosgrove

Editor: Salwa Jabado

Production Editor: Andrew Yackira

Photography © Marija Vidal, 2018; food styling by Cregg Green; © Melina Hammer, 2018, p. 2–3, 8–9; © Nicholas Gang, 2018, author photo.

Illustrations: alexandragl1/istock.com, anna42f/istock.com, eveleen/shutterstock.com, Hein Nouwens/shutterstock.com, Natalia Sheinkin/shutterstock.com

Recipe, page ii: Peanut Butter Surprise Brownie, *page 114.*

ISBN: Print 978-1-64152-135-2 | eBook 978-1-64152-136-9

To my two beautiful, funny, interesting kids: My daughter, Layla, a true kid chef, foodie, and the inspiration for all of the recipes in this book. My son, Ayan, who might be too young to cook, but is already having fun trying new foods! And to my husband and best friend, Niral, who has always believed in and supported me.

Alphabet Pretzel Sticks
with Cheesy Dip (page 88)

CONTENTS

A NOTE TO GROWN-UPS xi

A NOTE TO KIDS xiii

Chapter One
A KID'S KITCHEN 1

Chapter Two
BREAKFAST 11

Egg-cellent Muffin Cups 12

Blueberry Blast Banana Bread 16

Apple-Cinnamon French Toast Bake 20

Bunny Pancakes 24

Magic Unicorn Toast 28

Chapter Three

REAL MEALS 33

Pizza Party 34

Easy Peas-y Mac and Cheesy 38

Rainbow Veggie Pinwheels 42

Butterfly Quesadillas 46

Magic Wands 50

Lasagna Roll-ups 54

Turkey Sliders with Tricolor Fries 58

Goblin Green Pasta 62

Sunshine Soup 66

Burrito Boats 70

Chapter Four

SNACKS 75

Broccoli-Cheese Nuggets 76

Smashed Silly Face Guacamole 80

Treasure Trail Mix 84

Alphabet Pretzel Sticks with Cheesy Dip 88

Kale Chips 92

Chapter Five

DESSERTS 97

Cookie Bites 98

Tricolor Ice Pops 102

Fun Fruit Rolls 106

Strawberry Shortcakes 110

Peanut Butter Surprise Brownies 114

COOKING WITH KIDS 101: A GUIDE FOR GROWN-UPS 119

MEASUREMENT CONVERSIONS 123

RECIPE INDEX 124

INDEX 125

FOODIE DOODLES 130

Tricolor Ice Pops (page 102)

A NOTE TO GROWN-UPS

I remember when I first let my daughter, Layla, help me in the kitchen.
She was about 3½ years old and very interested in all the spices and ingredients
that went into the recipes I was cooking. She asked me if she could cut one of the
veggies, and initially, I hesitated. Would she have the dexterity to help without
cutting herself? Would it be safe for her to be near the stove? Did I have the right
tools to make her successful?

I decided to have her start small—I gave her ingredients to throw into the pot,
held her hand while she stirred the pot on the stove, and helped her measure out
spices and add them to recipes. Slowly she (and I!) grew more confident about
her cooking, and by the time she was about 4½, she was able to cut produce with
a kid-safe knife, stir and sauté on the stove, and mix ingredients for baking on her
own—all supervised, of course!

By allowing and ultimately empowering my daughter to cook, I was able to
witness all kinds of other benefits from these experiences: They gave me an
opportunity to spend quality time with her and create lasting memories, broad-
ened her palate, helped me encourage her to try new foods, and gave her a sense
of ownership and pride in her ability to make something tasty that the whole
family could enjoy.

The recipes in this book are all inspired by my experiences cooking with my
daughter. She has taste tested the recipes, so I can guarantee that they are kid
approved! The recipes range from easy to hard. The easy recipes are those that kids
can do pretty much on their own with some supervision and guidance—these don't
use sharp knives or contain difficult steps. Medium recipes require more grown-up
involvement and may include more complicated steps or use of the stove top or
oven. The hard recipes usually have more complicated steps and require the use
of knives and the stove top or oven. These designations will help you decide where
to start and let your child grow in the kitchen as they gain confidence and skills. Of
course, you can always make a hard recipe with your four-year-old child; just assign
them the tasks that don't have the 🛑 safety symbol before them.

If your child is a reader, let them explore the book and pick out recipes they'd
like to try. For younger kids, you may want to plan ahead, look through the book
with your child, read recipes aloud, and set a time to cook together. If your child

is anything like my daughter, they will likely want to make all the recipes "right now!" You might want to keep that in mind when you show them the book.

In chapter 1, "A Kid's Kitchen," you'll find guidance on kid-safe kitchen equipment and some helpful kitchen rules, but since you know your child best, you can set your own limits on what is safe for your child and what parts of the recipe you feel comfortable having them take the lead on.

Here are a few more tips to make cooking with your child a stress-free, fun, memorable experience that will set them up for a lifetime love of cooking:

- Approach the recipes as an activity. Focus on the process rather than the end result. If your child exclaims, "I made it myself!" or "It tastes great!" at the end, that's all that matters. These results don't have to look perfect.
- Plan to cook when you have time. This will result in the most relaxed and fun experience for both of you. Weekends and rainy days are great for this sort of activity.
- Allow your child to taste, smell, and touch things along the way. Cooking is an amazingly sensory experience!
- Give up some control. When safety isn't a concern, feel free to let your child take the lead.
- Start small and build on skills. Give kids tasks they can reasonably accomplish and feel successful about, then expand their repertoire of skills.
- Set expectations. Kids are naturally impatient, so when making recipes that might have a long baking or cooking time, let them know what to expect before getting started.
- Clean up along the way. This is a good habit for kids to learn, but it will also help prevent you from being left with a pile of dishes at the end of a recipe!
- Read the Cooking with Kids 101 guide (page 119) at the back of the book. There you'll find more tips on cooking with kids and how to teach cooking skills.

The more you cook together, the easier it will get until one day, they are cooking for you!

I hope you and your child(ren) enjoy this book and the recipes in it as much as my daughter and I have, and that it helps you create warm, long-lasting memories in the kitchen!

A NOTE TO KIDS

Welcome to the wonderful world of cooking! You have probably seen your parents or other grown-ups cooking in the kitchen, and you're so excited to try. Well, now it's your turn!

Whether you are already a trusty kitchen helper or totally new to cooking, this book is for you. In it, you will find 25 delicious recipes that you can make for breakfast, lunch, dinner, snacks, and dessert. Each recipe is rated easy, medium, or hard. This will give you an idea of how much you can do yourself. If you see a symbol, that means a grown-up should help or supervise. Other than that, how you make these recipes is up to you! In fact, you can personalize each of these recipes by adding the date you cooked it, your star rating, the names of anyone who helped make the recipe, and how you changed the recipe to make it your own.

I hope you and your family love the food you create and have lots of fun making them together in the kitchen. Are you ready? Let's get started!

RECIPE RATINGS KEY

Each recipe is rated from 1 to 3 oven mitts to give you a sense of how easy or hard they are and how much a grown-up may need to help.

EASY

Simple steps and no sharp knives (kid-safe or butter knife). You can do most of this on your own. May involve use of the oven.

MEDIUM

Medium oven mitt rating

More challenging steps. May include sharp knives, appliances, and stove top/oven instructions.

HARD

More complicated steps. Usually includes sharp knives, appliances, and stove top/oven instructions.

a kid's kitchen

Before you get started, the first step is to get to know your kitchen a little better. Once you know how to stay safe while cooking, and the right kitchen tools to use for every recipe, you'll be ready to whip up all kinds of dishes!

KITCHEN RULES

Kitchen rules are important because they keep us safe when we're cooking. Even grown-ups cut their fingers or get burned. It takes practice! Some of the rules you'll find in this book are about using knives and ovens, but they also include things like washing fruits and vegetables, setting up your work area, and knowing when to ask a grown-up for help.

Here are six important rules for any kitchen:

1. **Always cook with an adult.** Some steps need a grown-up's help. Those steps have this 🛑 symbol. That symbol means a grown-up may need to supervise or do those steps, like cooking on the stove, using the oven, or removing food from a food processor.

2. **Wash your hands.** Our hands carry germs, so handwashing is super important. Before you start cooking, wash your hands in warm, soapy water and scrub for 20 seconds (the amount of time it takes to sing "Twinkle, Twinkle, Little Star" twice).

NOTE TO GROWN-UPS

Now is a good time to go over any specific rules you have in your kitchen that may not be mentioned here.

3. **Wash fruits and vegetables.** Fruits and vegetables also have germs and dirt on them. Before you use them, wash them under running water and give them a gentle scrub. You can use your hands or a soft brush.

4. **Handle eggs and meat safely.** Raw eggs and raw meat may have harmful bacteria on them. Wash your hands after you touch raw eggs. Use a different knife and cutting board for raw meat. Always wash your hands before and after touching raw meat.

5. **Prepare your work area.** The first step is to clear off the counter where you'll be "prepping" your ingredients (getting them ready). Wipe the counter with a clean, wet cloth or sponge. Then bring all the ingredients and tools you'll be using to the work area.

6. **Clean as you go.** You don't want a big pile of dishes at the end! As you use spoons, pots, pans, and other kitchen tools, let them cool if needed and then put them into the dishwasher or wash them and put them away. This will save you time later.

COOKING EQUIPMENT

Cooking can be really easy when you have the right tools. These are the simple tools you need to create the recipes in this cookbook. Ask a grown-up to show you how to use these tools.

TOOLS & UTENSILS

Aluminum foil

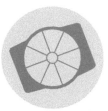

Apple slicer

Butter knife

Can opener

Child-safe knives (e.g., nylon knives)

Child-safe scissors (optional)

Colander or strainer

Cookie cutters

Cooking thermometer

Cutting board

Ice pop mold for 8 ice pops

Ladle

Measuring cups

Measuring spoons

Parchment paper

Pizza cutter

Potato masher (optional)

Rubber spatulas

Silicone mat

Timer

Tongs

Vegetable peeler

Wavy chopper crinkle-cut knife (optional)

Whisk

COOKWARE & BAKEWARE

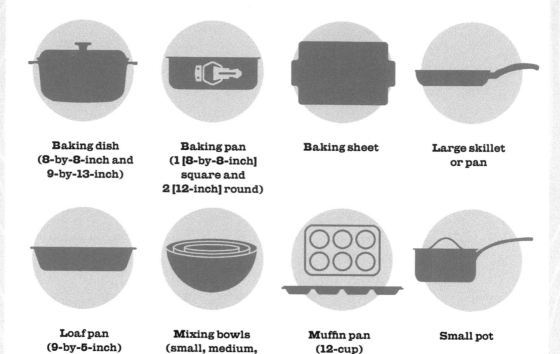

**Baking dish
(8-by-8-inch and
9-by-13-inch)**

**Baking pan
(1 [8-by-8-inch]
square and
2 [12-inch] round)**

Baking sheet

**Large skillet
or pan**

**Loaf pan
(9-by-5-inch)**

**Mixing bowls
(small, medium,
and large)**

**Muffin pan
(12-cup)**

Small pot

SMALL APPLIANCES

Blender

Electric mixer

Food processor

Hand (immersion) blender (optional)

COOKING CLASS

Recipes are directions to help you cook a dish or meal.

Here are six tips for reading a recipe, preparing your ingredients, and staying safe in the kitchen.

1. **Read the recipe.** Each recipe has a title that tells you what it is. The recipe also tells you the time it takes to make it, number of servings, list of ingredients, list of tools you will need, and directions for cooking. Before starting to cook, read through the whole recipe so you know what to expect along the way.

2. **Make sure you have all the ingredients.** Read through the list of ingredients, and make sure they're all already in your home. If not, make a grocery list and plan a trip to the store with a grown-up.

3. **Get out all the ingredients and tools.** It's helpful to take out the tools and ingredients you will need before starting to cook, so you're not looking for things in the kitchen while something is cooking on the stove!

4. **Measure carefully.** This is important for cooking, but really important for baking. Make sure all your spices and ingredients are measured level. (You can ask a grown-up to show you how to do this.)

5. **Be sharps safe.** Always have a grown-up with you when using sharp tools like knives, peelers, or graters. Before you start, talk with your grown-up helper about which tools you may use and how to safely use them.

6. **Be stove and oven safe.** When using the stove top or oven, it's very important to practice safety. Most of all:

   - NEVER start cooking without asking a grown-up.

   - NEVER touch the burners or a pan on the stove, because they might be hot.

   - NEVER leave the stove unattended when it's on.

   - NEVER leave an empty pan on a hot burner.

   - ALWAYS tie back long hair and roll up sleeves.

   - ALWAYS have a grown-up present when cooking.

   - ALWAYS use oven mitts to remove anything from the stove top or oven, or ask a grown-up for help.

Apple-Cinnamon
French Toast Bake
(page 20)

breakfast

Breakfast is the most important
and most FUN meal of the day!
Energize your body for the day
ahead with these tasty recipes.

egg-cellent muffin cups

Veggies, eggs, and cheese turn into tasty muffins that are perfect for a grab-and-go breakfast!

PREP TIME
20 minutes

COOK TIME
30 minutes

MAKES
12
SERVINGS

GLUTEN-FREE
NUT-FREE

KITCHEN TOOLS YOU WILL NEED

Measuring cups

Measuring spoons

Muffin tin

Cutting board

Kid-safe knife

Sharp knife

Medium bowl

Large bowl

Whisk

Wooden mixing spoon

Ladle

Butter knife

INGREDIENTS YOU WILL NEED

Olive oil or **butter**, for greasing the muffin tin

1 **Roma tomato**

1 **bell pepper**

6 ounces thick-cut deli **ham** (optional, leave out if vegetarian)

2 cups **baby spinach**

⅛ cup **red onion**

12 **eggs**

½ cup shredded **Cheddar cheese** (or any cheese)

½ cup **milk**

½ teaspoon **salt**

Pepper, to taste

**JUST FOR
LAUGHS**

**How did the egg
get up the hill?**

It scrambled up!

DIRECTIONS

1. Oil the muffin tin, and preheat the oven.
Use your fingers or a paper towel to spread
olive oil or butter all over the inside of the
muffin tin cups. 🛑 Preheat the oven to 350°F.

**2. Cut the veggies
and ham.** Using a
cutting board and
a kid-safe knife, cut
the tomato into
4 pieces. Then cut
the 4 large pieces
into small cubes.
Cut the bell pepper
in half. Take the
seeds out of the
bell pepper. Cut

the bell pepper into small cubes. If using ham,
cut it into small, bite-size pieces. Chop up the
baby spinach. 🛑 Using a sharp knife, peel and
mince ❋ the red onion.

❋ **Mince:** Chop
into very
small pieces.

MAKE IT YOUR OWN

Try different combinations for the muffin cups— use your favorite veggies, cheeses, and meats!

I MADE IT MY OWN BY:

- -

- -

- -

- -

- -

3. Beat the eggs, and stir the wet ingredients. In a medium bowl, crack 1 egg. Remove any shells, and pour the egg into a large bowl. Repeat with the next 11 eggs. Beat the eggs with a whisk until combined. Add the cheese, milk, salt, and pepper. Using a wooden spoon, stir until smooth. Mix the tomato, bell pepper, ham (if using), spinach, and onion into the egg mixture. With a ladle, scoop the mixture into the muffin tins, filling them three-quarters full.

4. Bake the muffins. 🛑 Bake in the oven for 25 to 30 minutes, until the eggs look solid and puff up. Let the muffins cool for a few minutes, then run a butter knife around the edge of each muffin to help lift it out of the tin. Serve warm.

blueberry blast banana bread

Banana bread is a great way to use spotty, overripe bananas. This recipe is moist and cake-like, so it makes for a yummy breakfast treat!

PREP TIME
20 minutes

COOK TIME
1 hour

MAKES
12
SERVINGS

NUT-FREE
VEGETARIAN

KITCHEN TOOLS YOU WILL NEED

Measuring cups

Measuring spoons

9-by-5-inch loaf pan

2 large bowls

2 medium bowls

Fork or potato masher

Whisk or fork

Rubber spatula or wooden mixing spoon

Kid-safe knife

INGREDIENTS YOU WILL NEED

Butter, for greasing the pan

2 large **eggs**

1 cup ripe **banana** (about 2 medium bananas)

1 cup **buttermilk**

⅓ cup **brown sugar**

⅔ cup **canola oil** (you can use half oil plus half **applesauce** if you like)

2 cups **whole-wheat flour**

1 cup old-fashioned **rolled oats**

2 teaspoons **baking powder**

1 teaspoon ground **cinnamon**

½ teaspoon **salt**

¼ teaspoon **baking soda**

1 cup **blueberries**

IT TASTED:
(CIRCLE
THE STARS)

★ ★ ★ ★ ★

WHO
HELPED?

JUST FOR
LAUGHS

**What did the blue-
berry say when he
made a new friend?**

Berry nice to
meet you!

DIRECTIONS

1. Oil the pan, and preheat the oven. Use your fingers or a paper towel to spread butter all over the inside of the loaf pan. 🛑 Preheat the oven to 375°F.

2. Measure and stir together the wet ingredients. In a medium bowl, crack 1 egg. Remove any shells, and pour the egg into a large bowl. Repeat with the second egg. In another medium bowl, mash the bananas with a fork or a potato masher. Add the bananas to the large bowl with the eggs, and stir. Add the buttermilk, brown sugar, and oil, and **whisk** * until blended.

❋ **Whisk: Use a
whisk or fork
to stir ingredients.**

3. Measure the dry ingredients, and mix all ingredients. In another large bowl, mix the flour, oats, baking powder, cinnamon, salt, and baking soda. Using a rubber spatula or wooden spoon, stir the flour mixture into the buttermilk mixture, mixing just until combined. Gently **fold** ✳ in the blueberries. Pour the batter into the greased loaf pan.

4. Bake the bread. 🛑 Bake for about 1 hour, or until the loaf is brown and a toothpick inserted into the center comes out clean. Cool in the pan for 15 minutes before cutting into slices and serving.

Instead of blue-berries, try other fruits in this yummy bread, like strawberries, pear, or apple!

I MADE IT MY OWN BY:

✳ **Fold:** Stir gently with a rubber spatula using a fold-ing motion, so it doesn't break or fall apart.

apple-cinnamon french toast bake 🧤🧤

Apple, cinnamon, and cream cheese melt into this yummy French toast.

PREP TIME
20 minutes
COOK TIME
45 minutes

MAKES
8 TO 10
SERVINGS

NUT-FREE
VEGETARIAN

KITCHEN TOOLS YOU WILL NEED

Measuring cups

Measuring spoons

Baking dish

Apple slicer

Cutting board

Kid-safe knife

Medium bowl

Large bowl

Rubber spatula or wooden mixing spoon

INGREDIENTS YOU WILL NEED

1 tablespoon room-temperature **butter**, plus more for greasing the baking dish

8 slices **whole-wheat bread**

1 medium **apple**

2 **eggs**

1¼ cups **milk**

4 ounces **cream cheese**, room temperature

2 tablespoons **maple syrup**

1 teaspoon **brown sugar**

¼ teaspoon ground **cinnamon**

¼ teaspoon **vanilla extract**

1 cup **strawberries, blueberries**, or other **berries** of choice, for serving

1 tablespoon **powdered sugar** (optional)

- - - - - - - - - - - - - - - - -

IT TASTED:
(CIRCLE
THE STARS)

WHO
HELPED?

- - - - - - - - - - - - - - - - -

- - - - - - - - - - - - - - - - -

- - - - - - - - - - - - - - - - -

JUST FOR
LAUGHS

**What kind of apple
isn't really an apple?**

A pineapple!

DIRECTIONS

1. Oil the pan, and preheat the oven. Use your fingers or a paper towel to spread butter all over the inside of the baking dish. 🛑 Preheat the oven to 350°F.

2. Cut up the bread and apple. Using a cutting board and a kid-safe knife, cut the bread into small cubes. Spread the bread pieces evenly to cover the bottom of the baking dish. 🛑 Core the apple with an apple slicer. Cut the apple into small pieces. Sprinkle the apple pieces over the bread.

3. Measure and stir together the wet ingredients. In a medium bowl, crack 1 egg. Remove any shells, and pour the egg into a large bowl. Repeat with the second egg. Add the milk, cream cheese, maple syrup, butter, brown sugar, cinnamon, and vanilla to the large bowl. Using a rubber spatula or wooden spoon, stir until smooth.

4. Add the mixture to the pan. Pour the wet mixture over the bread and apple. Stir everything around in the pan to make sure it's completely coated.

5. Bake the French toast. 🛑 Bake for 45 minutes. Once cooled, cut into small squares, top with the berries, sprinkle with powdered sugar (if using), and serve.

MAKE IT YOUR OWN

Use cookie cutters to cut the French toast into fun shapes, and top with fresh fruit.

I MADE IT MY OWN BY:

....

....

....

....

....

bunny pancakes

With a little creativity and practice, pancakes can be turned into all kinds of animal faces!

PREP TIME
15 minutes

COOK TIME
40 minutes

MAKES
8
SERVINGS

VEGETARIAN

KITCHEN TOOLS YOU WILL NEED

Measuring cups

Measuring spoons

Medium bowl

2 large bowls

Whisk or fork

Wooden mixing spoon

Large skillet or pan

Spatula

Butter knife

INGREDIENTS YOU WILL NEED

1¼ to 1½ cups **milk**, plus more if needed

2 tablespoons **canola oil** or **olive oil**, plus more for greasing the pan

1 tablespoon **honey**

1 teaspoon **vanilla extract**

2 **eggs**

1½ cups **oat flour** or **whole-wheat flour**

2 teaspoons **baking powder**

½ teaspoon **baking soda**

½ teaspoon **salt**

1 cup **blueberries**

2 tablespoons **slivered almonds**

Butter, for serving

Maple syrup (for serving, optional)

Heavy cream (for serving, optional, see Make It Your Own on page 27)

DIRECTIONS

1. Measure and mix the wet ingredients. In a large bowl, combine the milk, oil, honey, and vanilla and stir together. In a medium bowl, crack 1 egg. Remove any shells, and pour the egg into the large bowl with the milk mixture. Repeat with the second egg and **whisk** ✳ until the mixture is smooth.

2. Measure and mix the dry ingredients, and combine with wet ingredients. In another large bowl, mix the flour, baking powder, baking soda, and salt. Using a wooden spoon, gently stir the wet ingredients into the flour mixture until combined.

3. Oil the pan, and turn on the stove. Use a paper towel to rub oil into the bottom of a large skillet or pan. 🛑 Place the skillet on the stove top, and heat over medium-low heat.

✳ **Whisk:** Use a whisk or fork to stir ingredients.

4. Cook the pancakes.

(STOP) Pour about ¼ cup of batter onto the skillet for each pancake. If the batter is too thick, stir in a little milk in the batter to thin. Cook until bubbly on top and golden on the bottom, about 4 minutes. (STOP) Flip using a spatula, and cook until golden on the bottom, about 2 more minutes. Repeat with the remaining batter.

5. Make your bunnies!

Make two bunny ears by cutting two sections off the edges of a pancake with a butter knife or make two long and skinny pancakes. Make cheeks with two smaller pancakes. Place bunny ears on top of a whole pancake, add blueberries for the eyes and nose, the two smaller pancakes for cheeks, and slivered almonds for whiskers.

MAKE IT YOUR OWN

Try making your own butter by putting ¼ cup heavy cream into an airtight container and shaking it hard for 2 to 4 minutes, until the cream turns into butter. You can top your bunny pancakes with your homemade butter and maple syrup!

I MADE IT MY OWN BY:

----

magic unicorn toast

Rainbow food gives unicorns their magical powers. Eat the rainbow and maybe you can be magical, too!

PREP TIME
15 minutes

COOK TIME
10 minutes

MAKES

8

SERVINGS

NUT-FREE
VEGETARIAN

KITCHEN TOOLS YOU WILL NEED

Food processor

3 medium bowls

Wooden mixing spoon or rubber spatula

Toaster or toaster oven

Butter knife

INGREDIENTS YOU WILL NEED

1 (1- to 2-ounce) package **freeze-dried blueberries**

1 (1- to 2-ounce) package **freeze-dried strawberries**

1 (1- to 2-ounce) package **freeze-dried mangoes**

8 ounces **cream cheese**

8 slices **whole-wheat bread**

**I MADE THIS
RECIPE ON:**
(DATE)

IT TASTED:
(CIRCLE
THE STARS)

★ ★ ★ ★ ★

**WHO
HELPED?**

DIRECTIONS

1. Turn the fruit into powder in the food processor. 🛑 Add the freeze-dried blueberries to the food processor, and blend until the blueberries are a fine powder. Remove the blade, and pour the powder into a medium bowl. Carefully wipe the excess powder out of the processor bowl. 🛑 Replace the blade and repeat with the strawberries, then with the mangoes, pouring each powder into its own bowl.

2. Combine the fruit and cream cheese. Divide the cream cheese evenly among the three bowls of powdered fruit. Using a wooden spoon or rubber spatula, stir the cream cheese and each powder together until combined. Wipe the spoon clean between each mixture.

Try different
freeze-dried fruits
to make different
colors and flavors
in your rainbow.
You can also top
your toast with
fresh fruit.

I MADE IT MY OWN BY:

- - - - - - - - - - - - - - - - - - - -

- - - - - - - - - - - - - - - - - - - -

- - - - - - - - - - - - - - - - - - - -

- - - - - - - - - - - - - - - - - - - -

- - - - - - - - - - - - - - - - - - - -

3. **Toast the bread and assemble.** Toast
the bread lightly in a toaster or toaster oven.
Spread each cream cheese mixture on the
bread in a rainbow pattern: blueberry cream
cheese on the bottom, mango cream cheese in
the middle, and strawberry cream cheese on
the top. You can keep the colors separate or
use a butter knife to swirl them together.

Rainbow Veggie Pinwheels (page 42)

real meals

From homemade pizzas to quesadillas that turn into butterflies, you will have a blast creating all these recipes! These can all be made for lunch or dinner, and after making these, you'll be a pro in the kitchen.

pizza party 🧤🧤🧤

Making pizza dough from scratch is so much fun! Stretch and roll the dough and top with your favorite ingredients for a yummy meal.

PREP TIME
30 minutes

COOK TIME
10 minutes

MAKES
8
SERVINGS

NUT-FREE
VEGETARIAN

KITCHEN TOOLS YOU WILL NEED

Measuring cups

Measuring spoons

Cutting board

Kid-safe knife

Cooking thermometer

Small bowl

Whisk or fork

Food processor

Rolling pin

Ruler

2 (12-inch) round baking pans

Pizza cutter

INGREDIENTS YOU WILL NEED

1 **bell pepper** (optional)

4 **mushrooms** (optional)

1 handful **fresh basil**

1 cup **water**, heated to 110°F

1 tablespoon **sugar**

1 tablespoon **olive oil**, plus 2 teaspoons for coating the pans

2¼ teaspoons **instant yeast**

2¾ cups **whole-wheat flour** or **white whole-wheat flour**, plus more for dusting the work area

1 teaspoon **salt**

1 cup **pizza sauce**

2 cups shredded **mozzarella cheese**

¼ cup sliced **black olives** (optional)

I MADE THIS
RECIPE ON:
(DATE)

IT TASTED:
(CIRCLE
THE STARS)

★ ★ ★ ★ ★

WHO
HELPED?

JUST FOR
LAUGHS

What does an
anteater like
on its pizza?

Ant-chovies!

DIRECTIONS

1. Preheat the oven, and cut the veggies. 🛑 With a rack in the top half of the oven, preheat the oven to 500°F. Using a cutting board and a kid-safe knife, cut the bell pepper (if using) in half. Scoop out the seeds and cut the bell pepper into strips. Cut the mushrooms (if using) into small cubes. Tear the basil into small pieces with your hands.

2. Mix the dough ingredients. Use the cooking thermometer to check the water temperature. In a small bowl, **whisk** ✳ the warm water, sugar, oil, and yeast. Let it sit for 5 minutes. 🛑 In a food processor, combine the flour and salt. **Pulse** ✳ for 20 seconds, until combined. Slowly pour the water-yeast mixture into the food processor, and pulse until a ball forms, about 1 minute.

✳ **Whisk:** Use a whisk or fork to stir ingredients.

✳ **Pulse:** Press and release the pulse button on the food processor or blender to get a short burst of mixing.

3. Knead and roll out the dough. Spread about 1 tablespoon of flour onto a clean surface. (STOP) Remove the dough from the unplugged food processor, and place it on the floured surface. **Knead** * it until it comes together, about 2 minutes. (STOP) Divide the dough in half, and use a rolling pin to roll the dough into two circles. Use the ruler to measure them to about 10 inches across. Rub about 1 teaspoon of olive oil onto a round baking pan to lightly coat it (use more oil if needed). Use both hands to lift the dough into the baking pan. Repeat with the second dough round, the remaining teaspoon of oil, and the other round baking pan.

4. Top the pizzas and bake. Spread the pizza sauce onto the two rounds of dough. Top with the cheese, cut vegetables, basil, and olives (if using). (STOP) Bake on the top rack for about 12 minutes, until the crust and cheese are slightly golden. Let cool. (STOP) Use a pizza cutter to slice the pizza and serve.

MAKE IT YOUR OWN

You can use whole-wheat pita bread or English muffins as your pizza "dough" to make this recipe quicker or to create mini personal pizzas. Also, mix up the toppings with your favorite vegetables or precooked meats.

I MADE IT MY OWN BY:

....

....

....

....

....

* **Knead: Use hands to press and fold dough to help it combine and eventually rise.**

easy peas-y mac and cheesy

This mac and cheese tastes even better than the boxed stuff, with an ooey-gooey homemade Cheddar cheese sauce.

PREP TIME
20 minutes

COOK TIME
25 minutes

MAKES
8
SERVINGS

NUT-FREE
VEGETARIAN

KITCHEN TOOLS YOU WILL NEED

Measuring cups

Measuring spoons

Large pot

Colander

Large skillet or pan

Wooden mixing spoon

Whisk or fork

✳ **Divided:** This ingredient will be added at two different times during the cooking process.

INGREDIENTS YOU WILL NEED

8 ounces **whole-wheat macaroni**

1 teaspoon plus ¼ teaspoon **salt**, **divided**✳, plus more to taste

1 teaspoon **olive oil**

1 cup frozen **peas**

16 ounces pre-cut fresh **broccoli florets** (optional)

2 tablespoons **butter**

¼ cup **flour**

2 cups **milk**

1 cup **vegetable broth** or **chicken broth**

⅛ teaspoon **black pepper**, plus more to taste

2 cups shredded **Cheddar cheese**

¼ cup shredded **Parmesan cheese**

I MADE THIS RECIPE ON:
(DATE)

IT TASTED:
(CIRCLE THE STARS)

★ ★ ★ ★ ★

WHO HELPED?

JUST FOR LAUGHS

What do vegetables want more than anything?

World peas (peace)!

DIRECTIONS

1. Cook the pasta. Fill a large pot three-quarters full with water. Add the macaroni and 1 teaspoon of salt. 🛑 Heat the water on the stove top over high heat until boiling. Cook, following package directions, then drain in a colander.

2. Cook the vegetables. Coat a large skillet or pan with 1 teaspoon of olive oil. 🛑 Heat the pan on the stove top over medium heat. Add the peas and broccoli (if using), and cook for about 10 minutes, stirring with a wooden spoon, until tender.

3. Make the cheese sauce. 🛑 In the large pot over medium-low heat, melt the butter. Add the flour and, stirring constantly with a wooden spoon, cook for 2 minutes, or until the flour is pasty and golden. 🛑 Turn the heat up to medium-high. Add the milk and broth, and **whisk**✳. 🛑 Bring the mixture to a boil, whisking constantly. Continue cooking, whisking constantly, for about 5 minutes, or until the sauce becomes smooth and thick. Add the remaining ¼ teaspoon of salt and the pepper. Turn off the stove. Add the Cheddar cheese, and mix until the cheese is melted.

4. Combine the mac and cheese. Add the macaroni and vegetables to the cheese sauce in the pot, and stir until combined. Stir in the Parmesan cheese. Serve hot.

 Whisk: Use a whisk or fork to stir ingredients.

MAKE IT YOUR OWN

You can add 1 cup of pumpkin purée with the cheese. The pumpkin makes this dish creamier and a little sweet. Also, test out different mix-ins and veggie combinations! Roasted carrots, Brussels sprouts, caramelized onions, and garlic are a few favorite mac and cheese mix-ins in our house.

I MADE IT MY OWN BY:

- - - - - - - - - - - - - - - - - - - -

- - - - - - - - - - - - - - - - - - - -

NOTE TO GROWN-UPS

The pasta is added to the water before heating for safety's sake. If you prefer to add the pasta after the water is boiling, feel free to do this step for your child.

rainbow veggie pinwheels

Vegetables are so bright and colorful! The right mixture of veggies can make a food rainbow in these easy, no-cook wraps.

PREP TIME
20 minutes

MAKES
4
SERVINGS

NUT-FREE
VEGETARIAN

KITCHEN TOOLS YOU WILL NEED

Measuring spoons

Colander

Large cutting board

Sharp knife

Kid-safe knife

Vegetable peeler

Small bowl

Butter knife

24 toothpicks

INGREDIENTS YOU WILL NEED

1 **red bell pepper** (about 4 thin slices per wrap)

1 **yellow bell pepper** (about 4 thin slices per wrap)

Purple cabbage (about 5 thin slices per wrap)

1 **carrot** (about 4 matchstick-size pieces per wrap)

4 (6-inch) **whole-wheat tortillas**

8 tablespoons **cream cheese** or **hummus**

4 handfuls **baby spinach**

DIRECTIONS

1. Rinse and cut the veggies. Rinse the red and yellow bell pepper, cabbage, and carrot in a colander. Using a cutting board and a kid-safe knife, cut the red bell pepper in half and scoop out the seeds. Slice the red bell pepper into thin

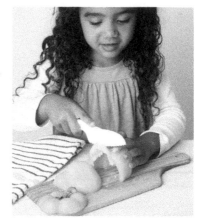

slices. Repeat with the yellow pepper. Slice the cabbage into thin slices. 🛑 Peel the carrot, and cut it into long, thin pieces (like matchsticks) or use the peeler to peel long, thin strips. Set the veggies aside in a small bowl.

2. Spread the cream cheese or hummus. Lay 1 tortilla flat on the cutting board. Use the butter knife to spread the cream cheese or hummus all over the tortilla.

3. Assemble the wrap.
Lay the sliced veggies and 1 handful of spinach flat in the middle of the tortilla. Beginning at one side, roll up the tortilla like a burrito.

4. Make the pinwheels.
Take 6 toothpicks, and stick them through the top of the wrap to the bottom, evenly spaced along the length of the wrap. Using your kid-safe knife, slice the wrap in between the toothpicks to create 6 pinwheels. Repeat steps 2 through 4 for the remaining tortillas and serve.

MAKE IT YOUR OWN

Try different veggies or even fruits (strawberries for red, blueberries for purple, etc.) to make different types of rainbows in this wrap. Enjoy any leftover veggies by dipping them in cream cheese or hummus, or use them in the next recipe, Butterfly Quesadillas (page 46)!

I MADE IT MY OWN BY:

---

butterfly quesadillas

With just a few extra veggies, you can turn plain old quesadillas into beautiful butterflies!

PREP TIME
20 minutes

COOK TIME
10 minutes

MAKES
1
SERVING

NUT-FREE
VEGETARIAN

KITCHEN TOOLS YOU WILL NEED

Measuring cups

Measuring spoons

Large skillet or pan

Large cutting board

Kid-safe knife

Kid-safe scissors (optional)

Plate

Butter knife

Spatula

INGREDIENTS YOU WILL NEED

1 teaspoon **olive oil**

½ small **tomato**

¼ **red** or **yellow bell pepper**

Handful **baby spinach**

1 **whole-wheat tortilla**

¼ cup **refried beans**

¼ cup shredded cooked **chicken** (optional)

⅛ cup shredded **Cheddar cheese**

1 **carrot stick**

1 small **grape tomato**

I MADE THIS
RECIPE ON:
(DATE)

....

IT TASTED:
(CIRCLE
THE STARS)

★ ★ ★ ★ ★

WHO
HELPED?

....

....

....

....

DIRECTIONS

1. Oil the pan, and cut the veggies. Use your fingers or a paper towel to spread the olive oil on the bottom of a large skillet or pan. Set the pan aside. On a cutting board, use a kid-safe knife to cut the tomato into small cubes. Cut 2 long slices of bell pepper, then cut the remaining bell pepper section into small cubes. Chop the baby spinach with the kid-safe knife or clean, kid-safe scissors.

2. Assemble the quesadilla. Lay the tortilla on a plate. With a butter knife, spread the refried beans on half of the tortilla, top the beans with the chopped veggies and cooked chicken (if using), and sprinkle the cheese on top of the veggies. Fold the tortilla in half.

3. Heat the pan, and cook the quesadilla.

(STOP) On the stove top over medium heat, heat the oiled pan. Carefully place the folded quesadilla in the pan. Cook for 5 minutes on one side, until the cheese has melted. (STOP) Using a spatula, flip the quesadilla over, and let it cook for another 5 minutes, until slightly golden brown and crispy.

4. Make the butterflies.

(STOP) Take the quesadilla off the stove, and cut it in half. On a plate, put the two halves with the pointy sides facing each other; these are the wings. Place a carrot stick between the halves for the butterfly's body. Place the grape tomato at the top end of the carrot stick for the butterfly's head. Place the two bell pepper slices on top of the tomato to make the butterfly's antennas. Enjoy!

MAKE IT YOUR OWN

For a sweet treat, fill your tortilla with cream cheese and fruit or peanut butter and bananas instead of veggies and beans. Experiment with different cut fruits to make your butterfly's body and head!

I MADE IT MY OWN BY:

....

....

....

....

magic wands 🧤🧤

Use your wizarding skills to create these delicious magic wand kebabs. They're so good, you'll put a spell on everyone you serve them to!

PREP TIME
45 minutes

COOK TIME
15 minutes

MAKES
12
SERVINGS

DAIRY-FREE
GLUTEN-FREE
NUT-FREE

KITCHEN TOOLS YOU WILL NEED

Measuring spoons

Colander

2 cutting boards

Kid-safe knife

2 large bowls

Sharp knife

Baking sheet

12 wooden skewers

Pan, for soaking skewers

Can opener

Plastic wrap

✳ **Divided: This ingredient will be added at two different times during the cooking process.**

INGREDIENTS YOU WILL NEED

2 **bell peppers**

1 pint **grape tomatoes** or **cherry tomatoes**

1 pound boneless, skinless **chicken breasts**

1 tablespoon plus 1 teaspoon **olive oil, divided** ✳

1 (8-ounce) can **pineapple chunks**, juice reserved (about ½ cup)

2 tablespoons **low-sodium soy sauce** (gluten-free if needed)

1 teaspoon minced **garlic**

Salt, to taste

Pepper, to taste

IT TASTED:
(CIRCLE
THE STARS)

★ ★ ★ ★ ★

WHO
HELPED?

- -

- -

- -

JUST FOR
LAUGHS

**What subject do
they teach at
wizard school?**

SpeLLing!

DIRECTIONS

1. Rinse and cut the vegetables. Rinse the bell peppers and grape tomatoes in a colander. On a cutting board with a kid-safe knife, cut the bell peppers in half, scoop out the seeds, and cut into 1-inch chunks. Place the bell peppers and tomatoes in a large bowl.

2. Cut the chicken. 🛑 Using the other cutting board and a clean sharp knife, cut the raw chicken into 1-inch bite-size pieces, and add to the bowl with the peppers and tomatoes. Put the cutting board and knife in the sink. Be careful not to touch anything else and wash your hands right away.

3. Preheat the oven, and prepare the pan and skewers. 🛑 Preheat the oven to 400°F. Use fingers or a paper towel to spread 1 teaspoon of olive oil all over a baking sheet. Place the skewers in a pan of water to soak.

❋ **Marinate:** Letting an ingredient sit in liquid before cooking for extra flavor.

4. Marinate ✳ **the veggies and chicken.** Open the can of pineapple chunks. Set a colander over a large bowl, and pour the contents of the pineapple can into the colander. Put the chunks in the bowl with the chicken and vegetables. In the large bowl with the pineapple juice, add the soy sauce, garlic, 1 tablespoon of olive oil, and salt and pepper to taste. Pour the soy sauce mixture over the bowl with the chicken and vegetables and stir. Cover with plastic wrap and refrigerate for 15 to 20 minutes.

5. **Assemble the magic wands.** Onto each skewer, spear, 1 bell pepper chunk, 1 piece of chicken, 1 pineapple chunk, and repeat 2 or 3 times. Top the wands with a tomato. Be careful not to touch anything else and wash your hands right away.

6. **Bake the magic wands.** Spread out the wands on the baking sheet. 🛑 Bake them in the oven for 15 minutes, until the chicken has cooked through, and serve.

MAKE IT YOUR OWN

Try different meat and veggie combinations for these magic wands! For example, shrimp, onion, and zucchini go great with a marinade ✳ of olive oil, lemon, and garlic!

I MADE IT MY OWN BY:

....

....

....

....

....

✳ **Marinade:** A liquid used to soak an ingredient before cooking for extra flavor.

lasagna roll-ups

These mini lasagna rolls are so much fun to eat! They are like little jelly rolls, but **savory*** instead of sweet.

PREP TIME
40 minutes
COOK TIME
30 minutes

MAKES
8 TO 10
SERVINGS

NUT-FREE
VEGETARIAN

KITCHEN TOOLS YOU WILL NEED

Measuring cups

Measuring spoons

8-by-8-inch baking dish

Large pot

Colander

Parchment paper* or aluminum foil

Cutting board

Kid-safe knife

Large skillet or pan

Wooden mixing spoon

* **Savory:** Salty or spicy, not sweet.

* **Parchment paper:** An oven-safe paper that keeps foods from sticking to the pan.

INGREDIENTS YOU WILL NEED

1 teaspoon **olive oil**, plus more for coating the pan

1¼ teaspoons **salt**, **divided***, plus more to taste

8 uncooked **whole-wheat lasagna noodles**

1 **red**, **orange**, or **yellow bell pepper**

1 **red onion**

4 **garlic cloves** (or 4 teaspoons pre-minced garlic)

1 (10-ounce) bag **frozen chopped spinach**

½ teaspoon **dried oregano**

⅛ teaspoon **crushed red pepper**

2 (20- to 25-ounce) jars **marinara sauce**, divided

½ cup **ricotta cheese**

1 cup shredded **mozzarella cheese**, divided

I MADE THIS
RECIPE ON:
(DATE)

....

IT TASTED:
(CIRCLE
THE STARS)

★ ★ ★ ★ ★

WHO
HELPED?

....

....

....

JUST FOR
LAUGHS

**What did the
shredded cheese say
when asked how he
was feeling?**

I'm doing grate!

DIRECTIONS

1. Oil the baking dish, and preheat the oven.
Using your fingers or a paper towel, rub 1 to
2 teaspoons of olive oil onto a baking dish until
it's well coated. 🛑 Preheat the oven to 450°F.

2. Cook the noodles. Fill
a large pot three-quarters
full with water. Add 1 teaspoon salt and the lasagna
noodles. 🛑 Bring the pot to
a boil over high heat, and
cook according to package
directions. Once the noo-
dles are cooked, drain in a
colander. Once cool enough to handle, spread
out each noodle on a flat surface covered with
parchment paper or aluminum foil.

3. Cook the filling. While the noodles cook,
rinse the bell pepper and onion. On a cutting
board with a kid-safe knife, chop the bell pepper
in half and remove the seeds. Chop the bell
pepper and onion into small pieces. **Mince** ✳
the garlic. Add 1 teaspoon of olive oil to a large
skillet. 🛑 Heat the pan over medium heat.

✳ **Mince:**
Chop into very
small pieces.

Add the garlic, spinach, bell pepper, onion, oregano, crushed red pepper, and ¼ teaspoon salt. Cook for 10 minutes, stirring often with a wooden spoon, until all ingredients have cooked through. Add 1 jar of marinara sauce to the pan. Cook, stirring, for another 5 minutes. Add the ricotta and ½ cup of mozzarella cheese to the mixture. Cook, stirring, for another 2 minutes, until combined.

4. **Assemble the roll-ups.** Spoon ¼ cup of the mixture onto one end of a noodle. Roll up and then place seam-side down in the baking dish. Repeat with each lasagna noodle. Once all the rolls are in the baking dish, pour the remaining jar of marinara sauce over the noodles. Sprinkle the tops with the remaining ½ cup of mozzarella cheese.

5. **Bake the roll-ups.** 🛑 Bake in the oven for 10 minutes, until the cheese has melted and is golden brown. Cool and serve.

MAKE IT YOUR OWN

Instead of marinara sauce, try other sauces like pesto or a cream sauce for your lasagna rolls. You can also skip the veggies and enjoy these roll-ups cheesy instead!

I MADE IT MY OWN BY:

NOTE TO GROWN-UPS

The pasta is added to the water before heating for safety's sake. If you prefer to add the pasta after the water is boiling, feel free to do this step for your child.

turkey sliders with tricolor fries

Purple, orange, and yellow fries make these burgers so much more fun!

PREP TIME
25 minutes
COOK TIME
25 minutes

MAKES
4
SERVINGS

NUT-FREE

KITCHEN TOOLS YOU WILL NEED

Measuring cups

Measuring spoons

Large baking sheet

Colander

Vegetable peeler

Cutting board

Wavy chopper crinkle-cut knife or kid-safe knife

Large bowl

Wooden mixing spoon (optional)

Rubber spatula or tongs

Medium bowl

Paper plate

Fork (optional)

Large skillet or pan

Sharp knife

Butter knife

INGREDIENTS YOU WILL NEED

2 tablespoons plus 1 teaspoon **olive oil**, **divided**✳

1 **sweet potato**

2 **yellow carrots**

2 **purple carrots**

1½ teaspoons **salt**, divided

¼ teaspoon **black pepper**, divided

1 teaspoon **garlic powder**, divided

1 tablespoon **seasoned bread crumbs**

1 **egg white**, beaten

12 ounces **ground turkey breast**

2 **tomatoes**

1 **avocado**

4 small **whole-wheat burger buns** or **dinner rolls**

4 slices **Cheddar cheese**

1 cup **baby spinach**, divided

✳ **Divided:** This ingredient will be added at two different times during the cooking process.

I MADE THIS
RECIPE ON:
(DATE)

IT TASTED:
(CIRCLE
THE STARS)

★ ★ ★ ★ ★

WHO
HELPED?

JUST FOR
LAUGHS

**What did the
hamburger parents
name their daughter?**

Patty!

DIRECTIONS

1. Oil the pan, and preheat the oven. Use your fingers or a paper towel to spread 1 teaspoon of olive oil all over a large baking sheet. 🛑 Preheat the oven to 400°F.

2. Rinse and cut the vegetables. 🛑 Rinse the sweet potato and carrots in a colander. 🛑 Peel the sweet potato with the vegetable peeler. Using a cutting board and a wavy chopper crinkle-cut knife or kid-safe knife, slice the sweet potato as thin as possible. Lay the slices flat, and cut each slice into short, wavy French fries. Peel the carrots, and cut them into wavy circles. Place the sweet potato fries and carrots in a large bowl.

3. Bake the fries. Add 1 tablespoon of olive oil, 1 teaspoon salt, ⅛ teaspoon pepper, and ½ teaspoon garlic powder to the bowl with the sweet potato fries and carrots. Toss with your hands or a wooden spoon to coat. Spread the fries on the baking sheet. 🛑 Bake in the oven for 20 to 25 minutes, gently tossing once with a rubber spatula or tongs halfway through cooking.

4. Make the sliders. In a medium bowl, mix together the bread crumbs, egg white, and the remaining ½ teaspoon of salt, ⅛ teaspoon of pepper, and ½ teaspoon of garlic powder. Add the turkey breast, and use your hands or a fork to mix until well combined. Shape the mixture into 4 patties, and place them on a paper plate. Put the mixing bowl and fork in the sink. Be careful not to touch anything else and wash your hands right away. (STOP) Add the remaining 1 tablespoon of oil to a large skillet over medium heat. Transfer the patties to the pan (and wash your hands again if necessary). Cook on one side for 5 to 7 minutes, flip with a spatula, and cook on the other side until cooked through and the inside is no longer pink, about 5 minutes more.

5. **Slice the toppings.** (STOP) With a sharp knife, slice the tomatoes as thinly as possible. (STOP) Cut the avocado in half lengthwise. Using a spoon, pop out the pit. Using a butter knife, slice the avocado inside the peel, and then slide the spoon between the peel and the flesh to remove the avocado chunks.

6. **Assemble the sliders.** On serving plates, open up each burger bun. Add the turkey burgers, then top each with 1 slice of cheese, ¼ cup of spinach, 1 slice of tomato, and some sliced avocado. Place the other half of the burger bun on top of the avocado. Serve with the fries.

goblin green pasta

Turn your pasta green with this tasty pesto sauce made from spinach, basil, and fresh herbs!

PREP TIME
20 minutes

COOK TIME
10 minutes

MAKES
8
SERVINGS

VEGETARIAN

KITCHEN TOOLS YOU WILL NEED

Measuring cups

Measuring spoons

Cutting board

Kid-safe knife

Food processor

Small bowl

Large pot

Colander

Divided: This ingredient will be added at two different times during the cooking process.

INGREDIENTS YOU WILL NEED

2 teaspoons **fresh oregano** (optional)

1 teaspoon **fresh thyme** (optional)

4 cups fresh **baby spinach**

¼ cup slivered **almonds**

¼ cup **fresh basil**

¼ teaspoon **black pepper**

2 large **garlic cloves**

2 tablespoons **vegetable broth** or **water**

1 tablespoon **olive oil**

2 teaspoons freshly squeezed **lemon juice**

1¼ teaspoons **salt**, **divided**

¼ cup shredded **Parmesan cheese**, divided

8 ounces uncooked **whole-wheat farfalle** (bowtie pasta)

Diced **tomatoes** (optional)

I MADE THIS
RECIPE ON:
(DATE)

- - - - - - - - - - - - - - - -

IT TASTED:
(CIRCLE
THE STARS)

★ ★ ★ ★ ★

WHO
HELPED?

- - - - - - - - - - - - - - - -

- - - - - - - - - - - - - - - -

- - - - - - - - - - - - - - - -

DIRECTIONS

1. Make the pesto sauce. 🛑 If using the oregano and thyme, use a cutting board and a kid-safe knife to chop enough oregano to fill a teaspoon twice and enough thyme to fill it once. Put the spinach, almonds, basil, oregano and thyme (if using), pepper, and garlic in a food processor. Process until chopped. Add the broth, oil, lemon juice, and ¼ teaspoon of salt, and process until well blended. 🛑 Carefully remove the blade. Spoon the sauce into a small bowl, and stir in half of the cheese.

2. Cook the pasta. Fill a large pot three-quarters full with water, and place on the stove. 🛑 Add the pasta and the remaining 1 teaspoon of salt, and bring to a boil over high heat. Cook according to package directions.

3. Combine the pasta and sauce. 🛑 Drain the pasta in a colander, then toss with the pesto. Top with the diced tomatoes (if using) and the remaining cheese, and serve.

MAKE IT YOUR OWN

Try different green veggies instead of spinach to make your pesto, like kale, parsley, or mixed greens!

I MADE IT MY OWN BY:

NOTE TO GROWN-UPS

The pasta is added to the water before heating for safety's sake. If you prefer to add the pasta after the water is boiling, feel free to do this step for your child.

sunshine soup

This orange soup is as bright as the sun! Top it with your favorite shredded cheese and enjoy it with some garlic bread for even more flavor.

PREP TIME
20 minutes

COOK TIME
45 minutes

MAKES
8
SERVINGS

NUT-FREE

KITCHEN TOOLS YOU WILL NEED

Measuring cups

Measuring spoons

Colander

Vegetable peeler

Cutting board

Large sharp knife

Kid-safe knife

Large pot

Wooden mixing spoon

Hand blender or regular blender

INGREDIENTS YOU WILL NEED

1 **butternut squash** or 2 pounds pre-cut **butternut squash**

½ **yellow onion**, diced

2 teaspoons **olive oil**

2 **garlic cloves**

3 or 4 **fresh thyme** sprigs

4 cups **vegetable stock** or **chicken stock**

½ teaspoon ground **cumin**

¼ teaspoon ground **nutmeg**

¼ teaspoon ground **cinnamon**

¼ teaspoon **black pepper**

¼ teaspoon **salt**, or more to taste

¼ cup shredded **Parmesan cheese**, or your cheese of choice (optional)

½ cup whole-wheat **croutons** (optional)

3 or 4 **fresh cilantro** springs (optional)

JUST FOR
LAUGHS

**What did one
snowman say
to the other?**

Do you smell
carrots?

DIRECTIONS

1. Rinse and cut the vegetables. In a colander, rinse the butternut squash. 🛑 Peel the butternut squash with a vegetable peeler. 🛑 Then, using a cutting board and a large sharp knife, cut off the top and bottom of the butternut squash. Then cut it in half lengthwise and scoop out the seeds, reserving them if desired (see Make It Your Own on the next page). Cut the squash into 1-inch cubes. Using a kid-safe knife, peel the onion and cut it into small cubes. **Mince** ✳ the garlic.

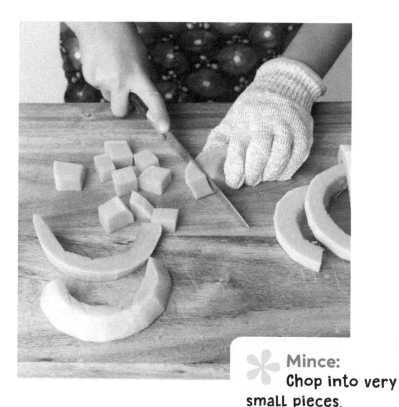

✳ **Mince:
Chop into very
small pieces.**

2. Cook the ingredients.

Add the olive oil to a large pot. (STOP) Heat the pot over medium-high heat. Add the butternut squash, onion, and garlic, and cook for 5 minutes, stirring with a wooden spoon. Add the thyme, stock, cumin, nutmeg, cinnamon, pepper, and salt to the pot. Bring the mixture to a boil, then reduce the heat to low, cover the pot, and **simmer** * for 30 minutes, or until the squash is tender.

3. Blend the soup.

(STOP) Using a hand blender, carefully purée the soup into a creamy, smooth consistency. You can also move the soup to a regular blender and blend until smooth. Be careful, since the soup will be very hot!

Serve topped with Parmesan cheese, croutons, and cilantro, if you like.

* **Simmer:** Cook just below the boiling point.

MAKE IT YOUR OWN

The butternut squash seeds can be roasted with a little olive oil and coarse salt, then sprinkled over the soup for a crunchy treat! To roast, (STOP) preheat the oven to 350°F. Spread the seeds on a baking sheet in an even layer, drizzle with olive oil, sprinkle with salt, and toss to coat. Bake for 10 to 20 minutes, until lightly golden brown, stirring halfway through toasting time to ensure even browning and checking frequently near the end to avoid burning.

I MADE IT MY OWN BY:

----

burrito boats

Did you know you can turn zucchini into little boats? This recipe is packed with tons of flavor!

PREP TIME
30 minutes
COOK TIME
40 minutes

MAKES
8
SERVINGS

GLUTEN-FREE
NUT-FREE
VEGETARIAN

KITCHEN TOOLS YOU WILL NEED

Measuring cups

Measuring spoons

9-by-13-inch baking dish

Colander

Cutting board

Sharp knife

Metal teaspoon or melon baller

Kid-safe knife

Medium skillet or pan

Can opener

Wooden mixing spoon

Aluminum foil

INGREDIENTS YOU WILL NEED

1 teaspoon **olive oil**, plus more for greasing the baking dish and zucchini

4 large **zucchini**

1 **red**, **yellow**, or **orange bell pepper**

½ **red onion**

1 (15-ounce) can **black beans**, drained and rinsed

½ cup canned diced **tomatoes**

½ cup frozen **corn**

2 teaspoons ground **cumin**

1 teaspoon **chili powder**

1 teaspoon **paprika**

¼ teaspoon **salt**, plus more to taste

1 cup shredded **Cheddar** or **Jack cheese**, or your cheese of choice

DIRECTIONS

1. Oil the pan and prep the vegetables.

🛑 Preheat the oven to 400°F. Using your fingers or a paper towel, rub a light coating of olive oil in a 9-by-13-inch baking dish. In a colander, rinse the zucchini. 🛑 On a cutting board, use a sharp knife to slice the zucchini in half lengthwise. Use a melon baller or teaspoon to scoop out the inside of the zucchini to hollow it out and turn it into a boat. Using your fingers, rub olive oil onto the inside of the zucchini. Place the zucchini skin-side down (hollow-side up) in the baking dish. Repeat with the remaining zucchini. Using a cutting board and a kid-safe knife, cut the bell pepper in half and remove the seeds. Cut the pepper into small cubes. Cut the onion into small cubes.

2. Cook the filling.

(STOP) Add 1 teaspoon of olive oil to a medium skillet or pan. Heat over medium heat. Open the can of black beans, drain them in a colander and rinse. Add the black beans, tomatoes, bell pepper, red onion, corn, cumin, chili powder, paprika, and salt. Stir with a wooden spoon, and cook for 5 to 10 minutes, stirring often, until the veggies are cooked through.

3. Fill the boats. Scoop the veggies into each of the zucchini boats until they are full. Top the boats with cheese. Cover the baking dish with aluminum foil.

4. Bake the boats. (STOP) Bake in the oven for 20 minutes. Remove the foil and cook for another 5 to 10 minutes. Cool and serve.

MAKE IT YOUR OWN

You can make boats with any kind of squash, like spaghetti squash or yellow squash. Mix up the toppings, too, with any veggies you like. You can also use shredded chicken or ground turkey in place of the black beans.

I MADE IT MY OWN BY:

Smashed Silly Face Guacamole (page 80)

snacks

Silly faces, food shaped like letters,
a treasure box of treats, and nuggets
that fit into the palm of your hands.
These snacks look more like toys than
food, but they all taste amazing and
are fun to make and eat!

broccoli-cheese nuggets

Crispy on the outside, cheesy and soft on the inside, these nuggets are the perfect after-school snack!

PREP TIME
10 minutes

COOK TIME
20 minutes

MAKES

8

SERVINGS

NUT-FREE
VEGETARIAN

KITCHEN TOOLS YOU WILL NEED

Measuring cups

Measuring spoons

Baking sheet

Medium bowl

Large bowl

Whisk or fork

Cutting board

Kid-safe knife

Wooden mixing spoon

INGREDIENTS YOU WILL NEED

1 teaspoon **olive oil**

2 **eggs**

2 **garlic cloves**

1 (16-ounce) package frozen **broccoli**, steamed

½ cup **whole-wheat bread crumbs**

½ cup shredded **Cheddar cheese**

I MADE THIS RECIPE ON:
(DATE)

IT TASTED:
(CIRCLE THE STARS)

★ ★ ★ ★ ★

WHO HELPED?

JUST FOR LAUGHS

What do you get when you cross broccoli with a vampire?

Count Brocula!

DIRECTIONS

1. Preheat the oven and crack the eggs.
(STOP) Preheat the oven to 400°F. Use your fingers or a paper towel to rub the olive oil all over a baking sheet. In a medium bowl, crack 1 egg. Remove any shells, and pour the egg into a

large bowl. Repeat with the second egg. Beat the eggs with a whisk or fork until smooth.

2. Chop and mix the ingredients. Using a cutting board and a kid-safe knife, **mince** ✳ the garlic. Chop the steamed broccoli into small pieces. Add the broccoli, bread crumbs, cheese, and garlic to the bowl with the eggs. Using a wooden spoon, mix well to combine.

✳ **Mince:** Chop into very small pieces.

3. Make the nuggets. Using your hands, take 1 tablespoon of the broccoli mixture and roll it into a ball or form it into a patty. Place it on the baking sheet. Repeat with the rest of the mixture, spreading all the nuggets out on the baking sheet.

4. Bake the nuggets. 🛑 Bake in the oven for about 20 minutes, or until lightly brown and crispy on top. Cool and serve.

smashed silly face guacamole

Guacamole and chips are even more fun by turning the bowl of guacamole into a silly face.

PREP TIME
20 minutes
COOK TIME
20 minutes

MAKES
8
SERVINGS

DAIRY-FREE
GLUTEN-FREE
NUT-FREE
VEGAN

KITCHEN TOOLS YOU WILL NEED

Measuring spoons

Baking sheet

Cutting board

Kid-safe knife

Spoon

Medium bowl

Fork or potato masher

Pizza cutter

Tongs

✳ Garnish: Something small added for decoration and/or flavor right before serving.

INGREDIENTS YOU WILL NEED

1 teaspoon **olive oil**, plus more or **olive oil spray** for greasing the baking sheet and rubbing the tortillas

2 **avocados**

1 **tomato**

¼ **red onion** (optional)

Juice of ½ **lime**, plus 2 **lime slices**, for **garnish** ✳

Salt, to taste

1 tablespoon **fresh cilantro**

1 package **corn tortillas** (about 8 tortillas)

1 **cherry tomato**, cut in half

1 slice **red onion**

I MADE THIS
RECIPE ON:
(DATE)

IT TASTED:
(CIRCLE
THE STARS)

★ ★ ★ ★ ★

WHO
HELPED?

DIRECTIONS

1. Preheat the oven, and cut the ingredients.
🛑 Preheat the oven to 350°F. Use fingers or a paper towel to rub the olive oil all over the baking sheet. On a cutting board with a kid-safe knife, cut the avocados in half lengthwise. Use a spoon to pop out the pits and scoop out the insides. Put the avocado pulp in a medium bowl, and set aside one pit for later. **Dice** ✳ the tomato and red onion (if using).

2. Mix the guacamole. Add the lime juice, salt, cilantro, tomato, and diced red onion (if using) to the bowl with the avocado. Mash with a fork or potato masher until combined.

3. **Make the tortilla chips.** 🛑 Using a pizza cutter, slice each tortilla into 8 triangles. Place the tortillas on the baking sheet, and spray with olive oil spray or rub with olive oil. Sprinkle salt over the tortillas. 🛑 Bake in the oven for 7 to 10 minutes. 🛑 Use tongs to gently turn the tortilla chips, and bake for another 7 to 8 minutes, until lightly brown and crispy.

4. **Make a silly face!** On top of the guacamole, add the 2 lime slices with 1 half of a cherry tomato on top of each lime slice for the eyes. Put the avocado pit you saved in the middle for the nose. Use the slice of red onion for the smile, add tortilla chips to the top for hair, and serve.

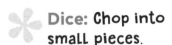

Dice: Chop into small pieces.

MAKE IT YOUR OWN

Experiment with different things to dip into your guacamole. Carrot sticks work great, and so do pita chips or even crackers. You can even try different ingredients to change your guacamole's facial expressions!

I MADE IT MY OWN BY:

....

....

....

....

....

treasure trail mix

Trail mix is sweet, crunchy, yummy, and so easy to make!

PREP TIME
10 minutes

COOK TIME
5 minutes

MAKES
10
SERVINGS

VEGETARIAN

KITCHEN TOOLS YOU WILL NEED

Measuring cups

Measuring spoons

Large bowl

Wooden mixing spoon

Zip-top bags or plastic containers

INGREDIENTS YOU WILL NEED

1 cup **whole-grain oat cereal** (like Cheerios)

1 cup **flake cereal** (like bran flakes)

1 cup mixed roasted, salted **nuts** (cashews, almonds, walnuts, and/ or pecans)

2 tablespoons **raisins**

¼ cup roasted, salted **sunflower seeds**

1 cup air-popped **popcorn**

½ cup **mini pretzels** or **mini whole-grain crackers**

¼ cup **mini dark chocolate chips** (optional)

I MADE THIS
RECIPE ON:
(DATE)

IT TASTED:
(CIRCLE
THE STARS)

WHO
HELPED?

JUST FOR
LAUGHS

**How much
does a pirate's
treasure cost?**

An arm and a Leg!

DIRECTIONS

1. Combine the ingredients.

Pour the measured ingredients—whole-grain cereal, flake cereal, nuts, raisins, sunflower seeds, popcorn, pretzels or crackers, and chocolate chips (if using)—together into a large bowl.

2. Mix the ingredients.

Using a wooden spoon, mix all the ingredients together.

3. Make the treasure boxes. Scoop ½ cup of trail mix into each of 10 zip-top bags or plastic containers to make your treasure boxes. Enjoy!

MAKE IT YOUR OWN

Did you know that trail mix can be anything you want it to be? Dried fruit, cereal, salty snacks—you name it! As long as the ingredients are dry and don't need to be refrigerated, you can add it into your mix!

I MADE IT MY OWN BY:

....

....

....

....

....

alphabet pretzel sticks with cheesy dip

You can spell your name and make a delicious snack all at the same time with these alphabet pretzels!

PREP TIME
25 minutes

COOK TIME
20 minutes

MAKES
12
SERVINGS

NUT-FREE
VEGETARIAN

KITCHEN TOOLS YOU WILL NEED

Measuring cup

Measuring spoons

Large baking sheet

Parchment paper *

Cooking thermometer

Large bowl

Whisk or fork

Wooden mixing spoon

Clean towel

Small pot

* **Parchment paper:** An oven-safe paper that keeps foods from sticking to the pan.

* **Divided:** This ingredient will be added at two different times during the cooking process.

INGREDIENTS YOU WILL NEED

1 package **active dry yeast** or **instant yeast**

1 ½ cups **water**, heated to 110°F

1 tablespoon plus 1 teaspoon **butter**, melted and cooled

1 tablespoon **sugar**

1 teaspoon **salt**, plus more for sprinkling

4 cups plus 1 ½ teaspoons **all-purpose flour** or **white whole-wheat flour, divided** *, plus more for flouring the work surface

Coarse salt, for topping

1 ½ teaspoons **butter**

½ cup **milk**

8 ounces shredded **Cheddar cheese**

½ teaspoon **mustard**

I MADE THIS
RECIPE ON:
(DATE)

IT TASTED:
(CIRCLE
THE STARS)

★ ★ ★ ★ ★

WHO
HELPED?

JUST FOR
LAUGHS

**What was
the pretzel's
favorite song?**

"The Twist,"
of course.

DIRECTIONS

1. Preheat the oven, and mix the dough.

🛑 Preheat the oven to 400°F. Line a baking sheet with parchment paper. Use the cooking thermometer to check the water temperature. Add the yeast and warm water to a large bowl, **whisk** ✳, and let sit for 1 minute. Add the butter, sugar, and salt to the yeast mixture. Mix well. Add the 4 cups of flour, 1 cup at a time, mixing in between, until the dough is no longer sticky and all the flour is mixed in.

2. Knead the dough.

On a clean, floured surface, **knead** ✳ the dough with your hands for 5 minutes. Shape it into a ball. Cover with a clean towel and let it rest for 10 minutes. Then separate the dough into 10 to 12 small balls.

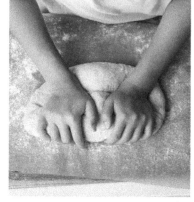

✳ **Whisk: Use a whisk or fork to stir ingredients.**

✳ **Knead: Use hands to press and fold dough to help it combine and eventually rise.**

3. Make the pretzel letters and bake. Take each ball and roll it back and forth with the palm of your hand into a long rope. Then form each rope into any letter or shape you like. Place the shaped pretzels on the baking sheet. With a wooden spoon, coat each pretzel with the melted butter, and sprinkle with salt. (STOP) Bake for 12 to 15 minutes, until golden brown on top.

4. Make the cheese sauce. In a small pot, combine the 1½ teaspoons of butter and the remaining 1½ teaspoons of flour. (STOP) Heat the pot over medium heat, and whisk the butter and flour together until they become foamy, about 5 minutes. Cook and whisk for about 1 minute. Add the milk to the pot, and keep whisking while turning the heat up to a **simmer** *. Keep stirring until the mixture is thick enough to coat the back of a spoon, about 5 minutes or so. Reduce the heat to low, and stir in the cheese until melted. Stir in the mustard, and let cook for 1 minute more. Serve with the pretzels.

MAKE IT YOUR OWN

Get creative! Write your name out with your pretzel ropes or try making pretzel numbers or silly shapes before baking.

I MADE IT MY OWN BY:

....

....

....

....

....

* **Simmer: Cook just below the boiling point.**

kale chips

These easy, crispy kale chips are a fun way to mix up snack time at home.

PREP TIME
10 minutes

COOK TIME
20 minutes

MAKES
8
SERVINGS

GLUTEN-FREE
NUT-FREE
VEGETARIAN

KITCHEN TOOLS YOU WILL NEED

Measuring cups

Measuring spoons

Cutting board

Kid-safe knife

Large bowl

Wooden mixing spoon

Baking sheet

INGREDIENTS YOU WILL NEED

2 bunches **kale**, washed and dried

2 teaspoons **olive oil**, plus more if needed

½ teaspoon **sea salt**, plus more to taste

¼ teaspoon **garlic powder** (optional)

¼ cup grated **Parmesan cheese** (optional)

JUST FOR
LAUGHS

**What do you call
a story about
vegetables?**

A fairy kale!

DIRECTIONS

1. Preheat the oven, and chop the vegetables.
🛑 Preheat the oven to 375°F. With a cutting board and a kid-safe knife, cut out the center stems of the kale. Roughly chop the kale leaves.

2. Season the chips. In a large bowl, combine the kale, olive oil, salt, and garlic (if using). Using a wooden spoon, mix until the kale is completely coated with the other ingredients.

3. **Bake the chips.** Spread the kale on a baking sheet. The kale does not need to be in a single layer, since it will shrink as it cooks. 🛑 Bake for 15 to 20 minutes, turning once or twice while cooking, until the leaves are crisp on the edges and slightly browned. Cool, add Parmesan cheese (if using), toss, and serve.

 MAKE IT YOUR OWN

Try different spices and seasonings on your kale chips! Garlic powder, chili powder, and paprika are some of our favorites.

I MADE IT MY OWN BY:

....

....

....

....

....

Strawberry Shortcakes (page 110)

desserts

Whether you like chocolatey, fruity, warm, or frozen treats, there's a dessert here for you. But you may want to sample them all before voting on your favorite!

cookie bites

These no-bake cookie bites will have you reaching into the cookie jar for more!

PREP TIME
10 minutes, plus 30 minutes to chill

MAKES
20
SERVINGS

DAIRY-FREE
GLUTEN-FREE
VEGETARIAN

KITCHEN TOOLS YOU WILL NEED

Measuring cups

Measuring spoons

Large bowl

Wooden mixing spoon

Baking sheet

Parchment paper *

Cookie scoop (optional)

* **Parchment paper:** An oven-safe paper that keeps foods from sticking to the pan.

* **Pinch:** A tiny bit of an ingredient; the amount you can pinch between your pointer finger and thumb.

INGREDIENTS YOU WILL NEED

1 cup **rolled oats** or **quick-cooking oats**

½ cup **peanut butter**

¼ cup **mini dark chocolate chips**

2 tablespoons **maple syrup**

¼ teaspoon **vanilla extract**

Pinch * **sea salt**

**When should a
cookie go to the
doctor?**

When it feels
crummy!

DIRECTIONS

1. Mix the ingredients.
In a large bowl, using a wooden spoon, stir together the oats, peanut butter, chocolate chips, maple syrup, vanilla, and salt, until combined.

2. Roll the cookie bites.
Line a baking sheet with parchment paper. Taking small handfuls of the mixture, roll them into small balls 1 to 2 inches in size or use a cookie scoop. Place them on the baking sheet.

3. **Chill the bites.** Refrigerate the bites for 30 minutes, or until solid. Store in an airtight container or zip-top bag and enjoy.

MAKE IT YOUR OWN

Try different mix-ins for your cookie bites! Almond butter or cashew butter tastes great in this recipe—even tahini would work in place of the peanut butter.

I MADE IT MY OWN BY:

tricolor ice pops

See and taste the rainbow with these sweet, multicolored ice pops. These frozen treats are perfect for a hot day!

PREP TIME
30 minutes, plus 7 hours to freeze

MAKES
8
SERVINGS

DAIRY-FREE
GLUTEN-FREE
NUT-FREE
VEGAN

KITCHEN TOOLS YOU WILL NEED

Measuring cups

Blender or hand blender

Ice pop mold for 8 ice pops

Cutting board

Sharp knife

INGREDIENTS YOU WILL NEED

1 cup frozen **mango chunks**

½ **banana**

1 **kiwi**

½ cup **honeydew melon**

1 handful **baby spinach**

5 frozen **strawberries**

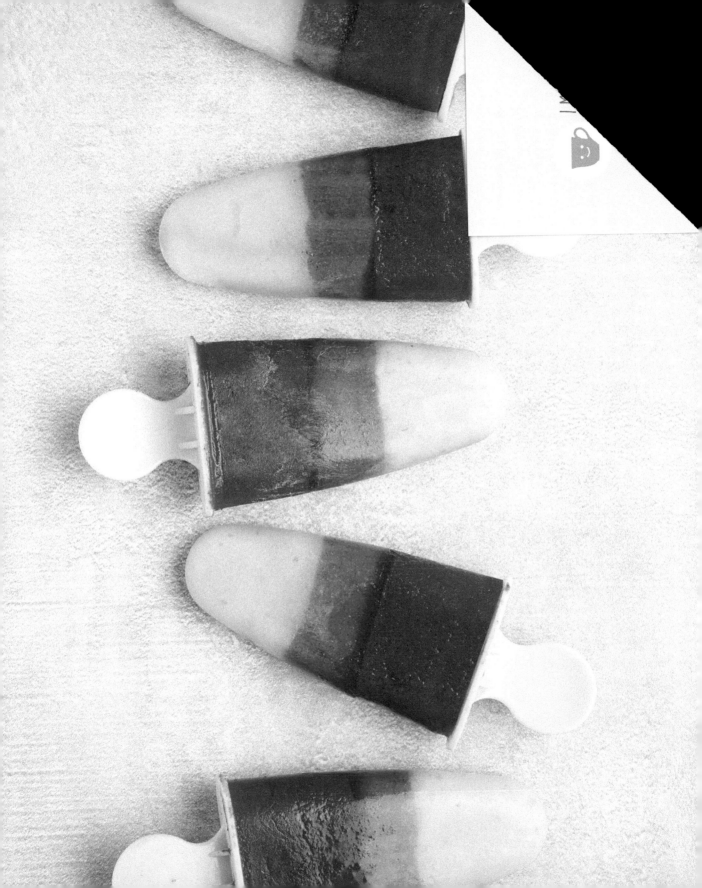

JUST FOR
LAUGHS

**What did one ice pop
say to the other
ice pop?**

Let's chill!

DIRECTIONS

1. Blend the yellow layer and freeze. 🛑 In a blender, or in a container with a hand blender, combine the mango, banana, and ½ cup water and blend. Add a little more water, if needed, to blend completely. Carefully pour the yellow layer into the ice pop molds, dividing it equally among the molds. Freeze for 30 minutes.

2. Peel the kiwi, blend the green layer, and freeze. 🛑 Use a cutting board and a sharp knife to peel the kiwi and cut a wedge of honeydew melon and chop it. 🛑 In the blender, combine the spinach, kiwi, and melon with ½ cup water and blend. Carefully pour the green layer into the ice pop molds, dividing it equally among the molds. Freeze for 30 minutes.

3. Blend the red layer and freeze. 🛑 In the blender, combine the strawberries and ¼ cup water and blend. Carefully pour the red layer into the ice pop molds, dividing it equally among the molds. Add the ice pop sticks and freeze for 4 to 6 hours, until completely set, and serve.

MAKE IT YOUR OWN

You can use any fruit in these ice pops for any color you want! Try blueberries for purple, oranges for orange, or even yogurt for white!

I MADE IT MY OWN BY:

----

fun fruit rolls

Unroll some fun and play with your food with these sweet, chewy fruit rolls! These are great as an anytime snack, or in bag lunches.

PREP TIME
30 minutes

COOK TIME
6 hours

MAKES
8
SERVINGS

DAIRY-FREE
GLUTEN-FREE
NUT-FREE
VEGETARIAN

KITCHEN TOOLS YOU WILL NEED

Measuring cups

Measuring spoons

Colander

Cutting board

Knife (type will depend on fruit chosen)

Food processor

Baking sheet

Silicone mat

Rubber spatula

Kid-safe scissors or pizza cutter

INGREDIENTS YOU WILL NEED

3 cups **fruit** (any kind—pick your favorite!)

1 tablespoon freshly squeezed **lemon juice**

1 tablespoon **honey**

DIRECTIONS

1. Process the fruit, and preheat the oven. Rinse the fruit in a colander. If necessary, use a cutting board and a knife to cut the fruit into smaller pieces. (STOP) In a food processor, combine all the fruit with the lemon juice and honey. Process until smooth. (STOP) Preheat the oven to 200°F.

2. Spread out the fruit. On a baking sheet lined with a silicone mat, pour the fruit mixture and use a rubber spatula to spread it out onto the silicone mat. Make sure the mixture is at least ¼ inch thick, especially around the edges.

3. **Bake the fruit.** 🛑 Bake in the oven for 4 to 6 hours, until the mixture has dried completely. Remove from the oven and let cool completely before cutting.

4. **Cut the rolls.**
Using clean kid-safe scissors, cut the rolls into strips. 🛑 If using a pizza cutter, first move the fruit from the silicone mat to a cutting board, then cut into strips. Roll each strip, and store them, refrigerated, in an airtight container for up to 1 month.

MAKE IT YOUR OWN
You can make this recipe with just about any fruit that comes to your imagination. The flavors are endless!

I MADE IT MY OWN BY:

- - - - - - - - - - - - - - -

- - - - - - - - - - - - - - -

- - - - - - - - - - - - - - -

- - - - - - - - - - - - - - -

- - - - - - - - - - - - - - -

strawberry shortcakes 🍦🍦🍦

Sweet straw-berries and fresh whipped cream make these little cakes irresistible!

PREP TIME
30 minutes

COOK TIME
15 minutes

MAKES
6
SERVINGS

NUT-FREE
VEGETARIAN

KITCHEN TOOLS YOU WILL NEED

Measuring cups

Measuring spoons

Food processor (or mix by hand)

Cutting board

Kid-safe knife

Medium bowl

Wooden mixing spoon

Baking sheet

Parchment paper ✳

Spoon

✳ **Parchment paper:** An oven-safe paper that keeps foods from sticking to the pan.

✳ **Divided:** This ingredient will be added at two different times during the cooking process.

INGREDIENTS YOU WILL NEED

1 cup **all-purpose flour**

½ cup **whole-wheat flour**

2½ teaspoons **baking powder**

½ teaspoon **baking soda**

4 tablespoons **sugar, divided** ✳

Pinch ✳ **salt**

4 ounces cold unsalted **butter**

½ cup **buttermilk**

¼ teaspoon **vanilla extract**

3 cups **strawberries**

1 teaspoon freshly squeezed **lemon juice**

Whipped cream, for assembling

Pinch: A tiny bit of an ingredient; the amount you can pinch between your pointer finger and thumb.

I MADE THIS
RECIPE ON:
(DATE)

- -

IT TASTED:
(CIRCLE
THE STARS)

WHO
HELPED?

- -

- -

- -

- -

DIRECTIONS

1. Preheat the oven, and mix the dry ingredients. (STOP) Preheat the oven to 425°F. In a food processor, combine the all-purpose flour, whole-wheat flour, baking powder, baking soda, 2 tablespoons of sugar, and salt. **Pulse** ✳ until combined.

2. Add the wet ingredients. Add the butter to the food processor, and pulse a few times, until the batter becomes crumbs. Add the buttermilk and vanilla, and pulse to combine. Set the dough aside.

3. Prepare the strawberries. Using a cutting board and a kid-safe knife, cut the strawberries into quarters. In a medium bowl, use a wooden spoon to stir together the strawberries, the remaining 2 tablespoons of sugar, and the lemon juice. Let sit for at least 30 minutes.

✳ **Pulse: Press and release the pulse button on the food processor or blender to get a short burst of mixing.**

4. **Make the biscuits.** Meanwhile, use your hands to separate the dough into 6 balls. Place them 2 inches apart on a baking sheet lined with parchment paper. 🛑 Bake in the oven for 15 minutes, or until lightly browned.

5. **Assemble the shortcakes.** After the biscuits have cooled, cut them in half horizontally. On the bottom half of each, spoon a dollop of whipped cream and strawberries. Top with the other half and serve.

MAKE IT YOUR OWN

Make your own whipped cream! In a large bowl, mix ½ cup cold heavy whipping cream, 1 tablespoon powdered sugar, and ¼ teaspoon vanilla extract with a hand-held mixer. Start on low speed, and slowly increase to high speed until soft peaks form. Mix-ins are great in whipped cream—try substituting orange or almond extract for the vanilla, adding a tablespoon of cocoa powder for chocolate whipped cream, or adding a small amount of strawberry juice to make the whipped cream pink!

I MADE IT MY OWN BY:

.

peanut butter surprise brownies

A peanut-y surprise lives inside these fudgy brownies!

PREP TIME
20 minutes
COOK TIME
35 minutes

MAKES
16
SERVINGS

VEGETARIAN

KITCHEN TOOLS YOU WILL NEED

Measuring cups

Measuring spoons

8-by-8-inch square baking pan

Large bowl

Medium bowl

Wooden mixing spoon

Fork

Rubber spatula

Toothpick

INGREDIENTS YOU WILL NEED

1 teaspoon melted **butter** or **olive oil**, for greasing the pan

¾ cup **all-purpose flour** or **white whole-wheat flour**

½ cup unsweetened **cocoa powder**

½ teaspoon **salt**

¼ teaspoon **baking soda**

2 large **eggs**

⅔ cup **brown sugar**

½ cup unsweetened **applesauce**

½ cup plain **Greek yogurt**

1 ounce **chocolate chips** or **dark chocolate chunks**, melted

2 tablespoons **canola oil**

¼ cup **peanut butter chips**

1 ounce **chocolate chips** or **dark chocolate chunks**, not melted

I MADE THIS
RECIPE ON:
(DATE)

....

IT TASTED:
(CIRCLE
THE STARS)

WHO
HELPED?

....

....

....

DIRECTIONS

1. Preheat the oven, and prepare the baking dish. 🛑 Preheat the oven to 350°F. Use your fingers or a paper towel to spread the melted butter or olive oil all over the inside of the baking pan.

2. Mix the ingredients.
In a large bowl, combine the flour, cocoa powder, salt, and baking soda. In a medium bowl, crack the eggs and beat them with a fork, then use a wooden spoon to stir in the brown sugar, applesauce, yogurt, melted chocolate chips or dark chocolate chunks, and oil.

MAKE IT
YOUR OWN

Add some colored sprinkles or chopped walnuts to the top before baking if you wish.

I MADE IT MY OWN BY:

----

3. Make the brownies. Pour the wet mixture into the dry mixture in the large bowl. Mix with a rubber spatula until combined, scraping down the sides as needed. Pour half of the brownie mixture into the baking pan. Sprinkle the peanut butter chips in a layer on top of the brownie mixture. Top with the remaining brownie mixture, and then sprinkle the remaining chocolate chips or chunks on top, spreading out evenly.

4. Bake the brownies. 🛑 Bake in the oven for 30 to 35 minutes, or until a toothpick comes out clean. Cool and serve.

COOKING WITH KIDS 101
A GUIDE FOR GROWN-UPS

Cooking with kids has so many benefits! It's a fun family activity, it helps picky eaters become open to new foods, and it helps children build ownership, self-esteem, and confidence in their abilities. It's also a great way to teach kids about where our food comes from, and how food affects the body, mind, and overall health. Here are a few tips and tricks to make the wonderful art of cooking with your children easy and safe.

KITCHEN HACKS

When I started cooking with my daughter, I gave her really small and discrete tasks that her four-year-old hands could handle. These tasks included things like using a butter knife to cut up a banana, tearing lettuce for a salad with her hands, or helping me stir ingredients in a pot on the stove (using a kitchen stool to reach the stove). As she grew more confident, I asked her to help me measure ingredients and allowed her to use a kid-safe knife to cut more challenging vegetables and fruits. I learned that giving her smaller tasks to start helped her build up the confidence to stick with some of the more challenging tasks later on without getting frustrated.

Here are some of the most effective cooking hacks I used when helping my daughter become a junior chef in the kitchen:

- If you don't have individual measuring cups, put a rubber band at the level you want kids to measure to.
- Have kids crack eggs into a separate bowl and fish out the shells. Once shells are removed, your little chef can pour the eggs into the bowl with the rest of the ingredients.

- Use bowls, pots, and pans that are bigger than needed, so there's extra room for a child's enthusiastic stirring.
- Practice knife skills with a banana and butter knife, and move on from there. You can even use a butter knife to cut lettuce, spinach, zucchini, and other soft vegetables.
- Set up a sturdy, nonslip stool so kids are the right height to reach things.
- Let your child always do any assembly required—it may not be perfect, but you'll have fun lavishing them with praise anyway!
- If thin slices of a vegetable are needed, your child can use a vegetable peeler instead of a knife.
- Use an apple slicer to core and slice an apple easily.
- Use a vegetable chopper to cut vegetables into small, diced cubes.
- If there are multiple kids, assign tasks ahead of time so everyone knows their job!

CHEAT SHEET FOR TEACHING SHARPS, STOVE TOP, AND OVEN SKILLS

When kids are cooking, of course nothing matters more than safety. Initially, I was worried about letting my daughter near a sharp knife, the stove top, and the oven, but I quickly realized that kitchen safety was an important skill for her to learn. With the proper tools and rules, you can set your child up for success and safety in the kitchen.

Real Knives vs. Kid-Safe Knives

When we talk about kid-safe knives, what exactly does that mean? Real knives are extremely sharp and sometimes quite heavy. Kid-safe knives are able to cut ingredients just like a real knife, but they are smaller, easy to hold, and often have a serrated but blunt tip so they can't nick anyone.

When your child is first starting out, you might want them to try a nylon serrated knife, which has the shape and feel of a chef's knife, but without the sharp edge. The blunt, serrated knife makes cutting ingredients possible without any risk of cuts to fingers. Or try a wavy chopper crinkle-cut knife, which cuts ingredients without a sharp blade (and creates a fun wavy pattern). But soon after your child masters that, you'll want to move to smaller real knives, like a paring knife. Real knives can cut tiny hands, so it's important to monitor your child closely when they're using them. If you are very concerned about cuts, you can purchase no-cut gloves for your child to use when handling knives.

Here are some tips for teaching your child knife skills:

- Have your child practice rocking the knife from tip to end when cutting. This will avoid the risk of the knife slipping.
- Teach your child to hold their non-knife holding fingers in a claw shape (keeping fingertips away from the blade), and to move their fingers and watch carefully as they move the knife down the ingredient.
- Explain that food is easier to cut when it has a flat, stable surface. Begin by cutting food in half or slicing off a part to create a flat side of the food to set your child up for safe cutting.
- Make sure your child is at the right height to get sufficient leverage over the food they are cutting. Use a nonslip stool if necessary.
- Build confidence by starting out with soft foods that are easy to cut and starting with a kid-safe knife or butter knife.

Graters and Peelers

The most important thing to emphasize when teaching children to use a box grater or a vegetable peeler is that these can be just as sharp as knives! It's important to take things slow.

Here are some tips for teaching skills with graters and peelers:

- Teach your child to grate and peel only in one direction (down or away from their body). When peeling, start with a long vegetable. Teach your child to hold one end of the vegetable in their non-dominant hand, and with their dominant hand, peel away from their body.
- Teach your child to grate using nice big pieces and stop before they get to the end of the ingredient. When grating cheese, keep it extra cold and have them grip it at the top, leaving plenty of room between fingers and the grater.
- When grating or peeling, describe it like petting a cat or dog—soft, gentle strokes. The softer the strokes, the softer any accidental skin contact will be with the grater.

Using the Stove Top

You may not feel comfortable letting your child use the stove top, and that's okay! This is a personal decision; you know your child best. But even if your child isn't using the stove on their own, it's still helpful for children to understand basic stove safety.

Here are some tips to teach your child about using the stove top:

- Tell them you use back burners first, so hot pots are further from the edge. Explain to your child that you always turn pot handles so they're not hanging over the stove top edge. This will prevent anyone from knocking into the pot and spilling it.
- Explain that you never leave a stove top unattended when it's on, and don't leave an empty pan on hot burners.
- Discuss the importance of checking for body safety: Tie back long hair, roll up long sleeves, keep loose clothing away from the stove, and be sure the kitchen stool and footwear are nonslip.
- Talk about the importance of being very careful with hot oil. Step back so it doesn't splatter on you.

Using the Oven

The same types of tips that apply to using the stove top also apply to the oven. Even if you won't be letting your child use the oven, you can still provide valuable lessons on how to be safe around an oven.

Here are some tips worth discussing when introducing oven skills:

- Emphasize never to touch oven racks with bare hands. Show that you keep plenty of heat-proof pot holders and oven mitts around, and show your child how to use them.
- Teach your child not to touch oven doors, as they can get hot as well.
- Explain how it's important to stand very far back when you open the oven door, especially when something may be steaming inside.
- Discuss the proper order for checking cooking progress: First, put oven mitts on, then open the oven door, and then pull out the oven rack to check for progress.
- Teach children to move slowly. When putting things in or taking them out of the oven, make sure everyone is moving slowly and there are no sudden movements, in order to avoid bumps or falls near an open oven.

MEASUREMENT CONVERSIONS

Volume Equivalents (LIQUID)

US STANDARD	US STANDARD (OUNCES)	METRIC (APPROXIMATE)
2 tablespoons	1 fl. oz.	30 mL
¼ cup	2 fl. oz.	60 mL
½ cup	4 fl. oz.	120 mL
1 cup	8 fl. oz.	240 mL
1½ cups	12 fl. oz.	355 mL
2 cups or 1 pint	16 fl. oz.	475 mL
4 cups or 1 quart	32 fl. oz.	1 L
1 gallon	128 fl. oz.	4 L

Volume Equivalents (DRY)

US STANDARD	METRIC (APPROXIMATE)
⅛ teaspoon	0.5 mL
¼ teaspoon	1 mL
½ teaspoon	2 mL
¾ teaspoon	4 mL
1 teaspoon	5 mL
1 tablespoon	15 mL
¼ cup	59 mL
⅓ cup	79 mL
½ cup	118 mL
⅔ cup	156 mL
¾ cup	177 mL
1 cup	235 mL
2 cups or 1 pint	475 mL
3 cups	700 mL
4 cups or 1 quart	1 L

Oven Temperatures

FAHRENHEIT (F)	CELSIUS (C) (APPROXIMATE)
250°	120°
300°	150°
325°	165°
350°	180°
375°	190°
400°	200°
425°	220°
450°	230°

Weight Equivalents

US STANDARD	METRIC (APPROXIMATE)
½ ounce	15 g
1 ounce	30 g
2 ounces	60 g
4 ounces	115 g
8 ounces	225 g
12 ounces	340 g
16 ounces or 1 pound	455 g

RECIPE INDEX

A

Alphabet Pretzel Sticks with Cheesy Dip, 88–91

Apple-Cinnamon French Toast Bake, 20–23

B

Blueberry Blast Banana Bread, 16–19

Broccoli-Cheese Nuggets, 76–79

Bunny Pancakes, 24–27

Burrito Boats, 70–73

Butterfly Quesadillas, 46–49

C

Cookie Bites, 98–101

E

Easy Peas-y Mac and Cheesy, 38–41

Egg-cellent Muffin Cups, 12–15

F

Fun Fruit Rolls, 106–109

G

Goblin Green Pasta, 62–65

K

Kale Chips, 92–95

L

Lasagna Roll-ups, 54–57

M

Magic Unicorn Toast, 28–31

Magic Wands, 50–53

P

Peanut Butter Surprise Brownies, 114–117

Pizza Party, 34–37

R

Rainbow Veggie Pinwheels, 42–45

S

Smashed Silly Face Guacamole, 80–83

Strawberry Shortcakes, 110–113

Sunshine Soup, 66–69

T

Treasure Trail Mix, 84–87

Tricolor Ice Pops, 102–105

Turkey Sliders with Tricolor Fries, 58–61

INDEX

. . . .

A

Almonds
  Bunny Pancakes, 24–27
  Goblin Green Pasta, 62–65
Apples
  Apple-Cinnamon French Toast Bake, 20–23
Avocados
  Smashed Silly Face Guacamole, 80–83
  Turkey Sliders with Tricolor Fries, 58–61

B

Bananas
  Blueberry Blast Banana Bread, 16–19
  Tricolor Ice Pops, 102–105
Basil
  Goblin Green Pasta, 62–65
  Pizza Party, 34–37
Beans
  Burrito Boats, 70–73
  Butterfly Quesadillas, 46–49
Bell peppers
  Burrito Boats, 70–73
  Butterfly Quesadillas, 46–49
  Egg-cellent Muffin Cups, 12–15
  Lasagna Roll-ups, 54–57
  Magic Wands, 50–53
  Pizza Party, 34–37
  Rainbow Veggie Pinwheels, 42–45
Berries
  Apple-Cinnamon French Toast Bake, 20–23
  Blueberry Blast Banana Bread, 16–19

Bunny Pancakes, 24–27
  Magic Unicorn Toast, 28–31
  Strawberry Shortcakes, 110–113
  Tricolor Ice Pops, 102–105
Bread
  Apple-Cinnamon French Toast Bake, 20–23
  Magic Unicorn Toast, 28–31
Broccoli
  Broccoli-Cheese Nuggets, 76–79
  Easy Peas-y Mac and Cheesy, 38–41
Buns
  Turkey Sliders with Tricolor Fries, 58–61
Buttermilk
  Blueberry Blast Banana Bread, 16–19
  Strawberry Shortcakes, 110–113
Butternut squash
  Sunshine Soup, 66–69

C

Cabbage
  Rainbow Veggie Pinwheels, 42–45
Carrots
  Butterfly Quesadillas, 46–49
  Rainbow Veggie Pinwheels, 42–45
  Turkey Sliders with Tricolor Fries, 58–61
Cereal
  Treasure Trail Mix, 84–87
Cheddar cheese
  Alphabet Pretzel Sticks with Cheesy
    Dip, 88–91
  Broccoli-Cheese Nuggets, 76–79

Cheddar cheese (continued)
    Burrito Boats, 70–73
    Butterfly Quesadillas, 46–49
    Easy Peas-y Mac and Cheesy, 38–41
    Egg-cellent Muffin Cups, 12–15
    Turkey Sliders with Tricolor Fries, 58–61
Cheese. See Cheddar cheese; Cream cheese;
    Mozzarella cheese; Ricotta cheese
Chicken
    Butterfly Quesadillas, 46–49
    Magic Wands, 50–53
Chocolate chips
    Cookie Bites, 98–101
    Peanut Butter Surprise Brownies, 114–117
    Treasure Trail Mix, 84–87
Cilantro
    Smashed Silly Face Guacamole, 80–83
    Sunshine Soup, 66–69
Cleaning, 3
Cooking equipment
    cookware and bakeware, 6
    small appliances, 7
    tools and utensils, 4–5
Corn
    Burrito Boats, 70–73
Cream cheese
    Apple-Cinnamon French Toast Bake, 20–23
    Magic Unicorn Toast, 28–31
    Rainbow Veggie Pinwheels, 42–45

D

Dairy-free
    Cookie Bites, 98–101
    Fun Fruit Rolls, 106–109
    Magic Wands, 50–53
    Smashed Silly Face Guacamole, 80–83
    Tricolor Ice Pops, 102–105

Dicing, 82
Dividing, 38

E

Eggs
    Apple-Cinnamon French Toast Bake, 20–23
    Blueberry Blast Banana Bread, 16–19
    Broccoli-Cheese Nuggets, 76–79
    Bunny Pancakes, 24–27
    Egg-cellent Muffin Cups, 12–15
    handling raw, 3
    Peanut Butter Surprise Brownies, 114–117
    Turkey Sliders with Tricolor Fries, 58–61

F

Folding, 19
Food safety, 3–4
Fruits. See also specific fruits
    Fun Fruit Rolls, 106–109
    washing, 3

G

Garlic
    Broccoli-Cheese Nuggets, 76–79
    Goblin Green Pasta, 62–65
    Lasagna Roll-ups, 54–57
    Magic Wands, 50–53
    Sunshine Soup, 66–69
Garnishing, 80
Gluten-free
    Burrito Boats, 70–73
    Cookie Bites, 98–101
    Egg-cellent Muffin Cups, 12–15
    Fun Fruit Rolls, 106–109
    Kale Chips, 92–95
    Magic Wands, 50–53
    Smashed Silly Face Guacamole, 80–83
    Tricolor Ice Pops, 102–105
Graters, 121
Grown-ups, cooking with, 2, 119–122

H

Ham
Egg-cellent Muffin Cups, 12–15
Handwashing, 2, 3
Honeydew melons
Tricolor Ice Pops, 102–105
Hummus
Rainbow Veggie Pinwheels, 42–45

K

Kale
Kale Chips, 92–95
Kitchen hacks, 119–120
Kitchen rules, 2–3
Kiwis
Tricolor Ice Pops, 102–105
Kneading, 37
Knives, 9, 120–121

L

Lemons and lemon juice
Fun Fruit Rolls, 106–109
Goblin Green Pasta, 62–65
Strawberry Shortcakes, 110–113
Limes and lime juice
Smashed Silly Face Guacamole, 80–83

M

Mangoes
Magic Unicorn Toast, 28–31
Tricolor Ice Pops, 102–105
Marinade, 53
Marinating, 52
Measuring, 9
Meat, handling raw, 3
Milk. *See also* Buttermilk
Alphabet Pretzel Sticks with
Cheesy Dip, 88–91
Apple-Cinnamon French Toast
Bake, 20–23
Bunny Pancakes, 24–27
Easy Peas-y Mac and Cheesy, 38–41
Egg-cellent Muffin Cups, 12–15
Mincing, 14
Mozzarella cheese
Lasagna Roll-ups, 54–57
Pizza Party, 34–37
Mushrooms
Pizza Party, 34–37

N

Nut-free
Alphabet Pretzel Sticks with Cheesy
Dip, 88–91
Apple-Cinnamon French Toast Bake, 20–23
Blueberry Blast Banana Bread, 16–19
Broccoli-Cheese Nuggets, 76–79
Burrito Boats, 70–73
Butterfly Quesadillas, 46–49
Easy Peas-y Mac and Cheesy, 38–41
Egg-cellent Muffin Cups, 12–15
Fun Fruit Rolls, 106–109
Kale Chips, 92–95
Lasagna Roll-ups, 54–57
Magic Unicorn Toast, 28–31
Magic Wands, 50–53
Pizza Party, 34–37
Rainbow Veggie Pinwheels, 42–45
Smashed Silly Face Guacamole, 80–83
Strawberry Shortcakes, 110–113
Sunshine Soup, 66–69
Tricolor Ice Pops, 102–105
Turkey Sliders with Tricolor Fries, 58–61
Nuts
Bunny Pancakes, 24–27
Goblin Green Pasta, 62–65
Treasure Trail Mix, 84–87

O

Oats
  Blueberry Blast Banana Bread, 16–19
  Cookie Bites, 98–101
Olives
  Pizza Party, 34–37
Onions
  Burrito Boats, 70–73
  Egg-cellent Muffin Cups, 12–15
  Lasagna Roll-ups, 54–57
  Smashed Silly Face Guacamole, 80–83
  Sunshine Soup, 66–69
Oregano
  Goblin Green Pasta, 62–65
Ovens, 9, 122

P

Parchment paper, 54
Parmesan cheese
  Easy Peas-y Mac and Cheesy, 38–41
  Goblin Green Pasta, 62–65
  Kale Chips, 92–95
  Sunshine Soup, 66–69
Pasta
  Easy Peas-y Mac and Cheesy, 38–41
  Goblin Green Pasta, 62–65
  Lasagna Roll-ups, 54–57
Peanut butter
  Cookie Bites, 98–101
Peanut butter chips
  Peanut Butter Surprise Brownies, 114–117
Peas
  Easy Peas-y Mac and Cheesy, 38–41
Peelers, 121
Pinch, 98

Pineapple
  Magic Wands, 50–53
Popcorn
  Treasure Trail Mix, 84–87
Prepping, 3, 8
Pretzels
  Treasure Trail Mix, 84–87
Pulsing, 36

R

Raisins
  Treasure Trail Mix, 84–87
Recipes, 8–9
Ricotta cheese
  Lasagna Roll-ups, 54–57

S

Safety
  food, 3
  sharps, 9, 120–121
  stoves and ovens, 9, 122
Savory, 54
Simmering, 69
Spinach
  Butterfly Quesadillas, 46–49
  Egg-cellent Muffin Cups, 12–15
  Goblin Green Pasta, 62–65
  Lasagna Roll-ups, 54–57
  Rainbow Veggie Pinwheels, 42–45
  Tricolor Ice Pops, 102–105
  Turkey Sliders with Tricolor Fries, 58–61
Stop symbol, 2
Stoves, 9, 122
Sunflower seeds
  Treasure Trail Mix, 84–87
Sweet potatoes
  Turkey Sliders with Tricolor Fries, 58–61

T

Thyme
   Goblin Green Pasta, 62–65
   Sunshine Soup, 66–69
Tomatoes
   Burrito Boats, 70–73
   Butterfly Quesadillas, 46–49
   Egg-cellent Muffin Cups, 12–15
   Goblin Green Pasta, 62–65
   Magic Wands, 50–53
   Smashed Silly Face Guacamole, 80–83
   Turkey Sliders with Tricolor Fries, 58–61
Tortillas
   Butterfly Quesadillas, 46–49
   Rainbow Veggie Pinwheels, 42–45
   Smashed Silly Face Guacamole, 80–83
Turkey
   Turkey Sliders with Tricolor Fries, 58–61

V

Vegan
   Smashed Silly Face Guacamole, 80–83
   Tricolor Ice Pops, 102–105
Vegetables. See also specific vegetables
   washing, 3
Vegetarian
   Alphabet Pretzel Sticks with Cheesy
      Dip, 88–91
   Apple-Cinnamon French Toast Bake, 20–23
   Blueberry Blast Banana Bread, 16–19
   Broccoli-Cheese Nuggets, 76–79
   Bunny Pancakes, 24–27

   Burrito Boats, 70–73
   Butterfly Quesadillas, 46–49
   Cookie Bites, 98–101
   Easy Peas-y Mac and Cheesy, 38–41
   Fun Fruit Rolls, 106–109
   Goblin Green Pasta, 62–65
   Kale Chips, 92–95
   Lasagna Roll-ups, 54–57
   Magic Unicorn Toast, 28–31
   Peanut Butter Surprise Brownies, 114–117
   Pizza Party, 34–37
   Rainbow Veggie Pinwheels, 42–45
   Strawberry Shortcakes, 110–113
   Treasure Trail Mix, 84–87

W

Washing
   fruits and vegetables, 3
   hands, 2, 3
Whipped cream
   Strawberry Shortcakes, 110–113
Whisking, 18
Work area, cleaning, 3

Y

Yeast
   Alphabet Pretzel Sticks with Cheesy
      Dip, 88–91
   Pizza Party, 34–37

Z

Zucchini
   Burrito Boats, 70–73

foodie doodles!

This is a drawing of my favorite recipe.

This is a drawing of _____ and I
cooking together.

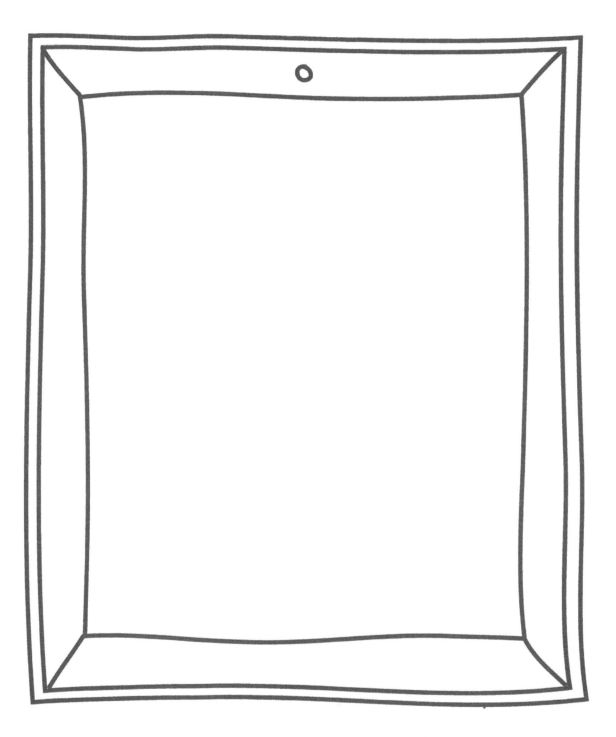

This is a drawing of my family.

In my imaginary garden, _____ grows.

ACKNOWLEDGMENTS

Thank you to my husband, Niral, for being a great partner, my biggest cheerleader, and my best friend through this entire journey. Thank you for encouraging me to follow my dreams and pushing me to experiment in the kitchen even when I wasn't confident I could create anything edible for us to eat! To my daughter, Layla, thank you for being my little taste tester and my "executive chef" in the kitchen. You are the most adventurous and curious eater, and so much fun to cook with! Watching you grow and learn has been amazing, and I cherish our time in the kitchen together, creating recipes for all of us to enjoy. To my son, Ayan, you are so new to food but are already very opinionated about the meals we have! I love your independence, and you are a little foodie in your own way. I couldn't be luckier to have all of you in my life.

To all of my readers of *The Picky Eater*: Thank you for sharing your experiences in healthy cooking with me, and for making what I do so rewarding. Your e-mails, comments, and messages about how my blog has helped you mean the world to me!

To my amazing editor, Salwa Jabado, thank you for being such a wonderful collaborator with helpful feedback and a flexible approach. To the entire Callisto Media team: Vanessa Putt, Patty Consolazio, Andrew Yackira, Liz Cosgrove, Amy King, Karen Beard, Marija Vidal, Kim Ciabattari, Melissa Reinhardt, Lucile Culver, Alyssa Nassner, and Eli Becker—thank you for all of your work, and for being so easy and fun to partner with!

To all of my dear friends, thank you for being there for me, laughing with me, commiserating about our kids and experiences in parenting together, and lending a listening ear when I've needed it.

And of course, to my family: Dad (Baba), my late mom (Mommy), and Nikhil. I bet you never thought the girl who didn't know how to use a can opener would build a career and life around food! Thank you for always supporting me no matter what path I've chosen, and for raising me to love and appreciate healthy, wholesome, flavorful food.

ABOUT THE AUTHOR

 **Anjali Shah** is a food writer, author of *Super Easy Baby Food Cookbook*, board-certified health coach, nutritionist, and owner of *The Picky Eater*, a healthy food and lifestyle blog. She is a mom of two who is a passionate advocate for healthy, clean eating for individuals and families. Her work has garnered nationwide attention, as she has been featured on Oprah.com, *Women's Health, Cooking Light, Reader's Digest*, CNN, Food Network, *SELF, Glamour*, BuzzFeed, *Huffington Post, Ladies' Home Journal*, Whole Foods, *SHAPE*, and at Kaiser Permanente. Anjali grew up a "whole wheat" girl, but married a "white bread" kind of guy. Hoping to prove that nutritious food could in fact be delicious and desirable, she taught herself how to cook and successfully transformed her husband's eating habits from a diet of frozen pizzas and Taco Bell to her healthy and flavorful recipes made with simple, wholesome ingredients. Through her blog, *The Picky Eater*, Anjali shares her passion for tasty, healthy cooking. When she isn't working with clients or media outlets, Anjali can be found playing with (or cooking with!) her daughter, Layla, and son, Ayan; spending time with her husband, Niral; or testing out new, healthy, family-friendly recipes for her blog.

discover more in the
kid chef
series

Kid Chef
**The Foodie Kids' Cookbook:
Healthy Recipes and Culinary
Skills for the New Cook
in the Kitchen**

Melina Hammer

978-1-94345-120-3
$15.99 US / $19.99 CAN

Kid Chef Bakes
**The Kids' Cookbook
for Aspiring Bakers**

Lisa Huff

97R-1-62315-942-9
$14.99 US / $19.99 CAN

CPSIA information can be obtained
at www.ICGtesting.com
Printed in the USA
BVHW091403121218
535448BV00028B/2046/P